SCHOLASTIC

National Curriculum
ENGLISH
Teacher's

PLANNING & ASSESSMENT GUIDE

Years 5–6

Key Stage 2

Scholastic Education, an imprint of Scholastic Ltd
Book End, Range Road, Witney, Oxfordshire, OX29 0YD
Registered office: Westfield Road, Southam,
Warwickshire CV47 0RA
www.scholastic.co.uk

© 2016, Scholastic Ltd

123456789   6789012345

British Library Cataloguing-in-Publication Data
A catalogue record for this book is available from the British Library.
ISBN 978-1-407-16019-1

Printed and bound by Ashford Colour Press

All rights reserved. This book is sold subject to the condition that it shall not, by way of trade or otherwise, be lent, hired out or otherwise circulated without the publisher's prior consent in any form of binding or cover other than that in which it is published and without a similar condition, including this condition, being imposed upon the subsequent purchaser.

No part of this publication may be reproduced, stored in a retrieval system, or transmitted, in any form or by any means, electronic, mechanical, photocopying, recording or otherwise, other than for the purposes described in the content of this product, without the prior permission of the publisher. This product remains in copyright.

Due to the nature of the web we cannot guarantee the content or links of any site mentioned. We strongly recommend that teachers check websites before using them in the classroom.

Every effort has been made to trace copyright holders for the works reproduced in this book, and the publishers apologise for any inadvertent omissions.

Extracts from *National Curriculum for England, English Programme of Study* © Crown Copyright. Reproduced under the terms of the Open Government Licence (OGL). www.nationalarchives.gov.uk/doc/open-government-licence/version/3/

Author Dave Cryer
Editorial Rachel Morgan, Jenny Wilcox, Rebecca Rothwell and Niamh O'Carroll
Cover and Series Design Neil Salt and Nicolle Thomas
Layout Andrea Lewis
CD-ROM Development Hannah Barnett, Phil Crothers and MWA Technologies Private Ltd

Recommended system requirements:
Windows: XP (Service Pack 3), Vista (Service Pack 2), Windows 7, Windows 8 and Windows 10 with 2.33GHz processor
Mac: OS 10.6 to 10.10 with Intel Core™ Duo processor
1GB RAM (recommended)
1024 x 768 Screen resolution
CD-ROM drive (24x speed recommended)
Adobe Reader (version 9 recommended for Mac users)
Microsoft Word

For all technical support queries (including no CD drive), please phone Scholastic Customer Services on 0845 6039091.

Table of Contents Year 5

About the Planning and Assessment Guides...... 5
About the Textbooks 6
Tracking progress... 7
Year 5 Curriculum links... 8

Grammatical words

Noun phrases 12
Perfect form of verbs 14
Modal verbs and Adverbs of possibility 16
Relative clauses 18

Punctuation

Commas to clarify meaning 20
Parenthesis 22
Using hyphens 24
Using a colon 26
Bullet points 27

Vocabulary

Prefixes: 'dis' or 'mis'? and
Prefixes: 're', 'de', 'over' 28
Suffixes: 'ate' and Suffixes: 'ify', 'ise' 30
Suffixes: 'able' and 'ably' and
Suffixes: 'ible' and 'ibly' 32
Adding suffixes to words ending 'fer' 34

Spelling

'ie' or 'ei'? 35
Letter strings: 'ough' 36
Silent letters 37
Words ending 'cious' and 'tious' 38
Words ending 'cial' or 'tial' 39
Word endings 'ant', 'ance', 'ancy', 'ent',
'ence', 'ency' 40
Homophones 41
Tricky words 42
Using dictionaries 44

Reading

Identifying main ideas and Identifying key details 46
Summarising main ideas 48
Predicting what might happen 49
Retrieving and recording information 50
Making comparisons 52
Themes and conventions 54
Fact and opinion 56
Explaining and justifying inferences 58
Words in context and Exploring words in context 60
How writers use language 62
Enhancing meaning: figurative language 64
Features of text and Text features
contributing to meaning 66
Asking questions and Answering questions 68

Writing

Planning writing 70
Headings and subheadings 72
Getting the verbs right 73
Making our writing flow 74
Adverbs and adverbials 76
Choosing the right word 77
Settings and atmosphere 78
Describing characters and using dialogue 80
Editing our work 82
Proofreading 84
Précising longer passages 86

Year 5 answers 178

Table of Contents Year 6

About the Planning and Assessment Guides 5
About the Textbooks 6
Tracking progress 7
Year 6 Curriculum links 10

Grammatical words

Using expanded noun phrases 88
Verbs: present perfect and past perfect tense 90
Relative clauses 91
Modal verbs and Adverbs of possibility 92
Subjects and objects 94
Active and passive verbs 96
The subjunctive 98

Punctuation

Commas to clarify meaning 100
Question tags 101
Hyphens 102
Bullet points 103
Colons and semi-colons in lists 104
Separating independent clauses 106
Parenthesis 108

Vocabulary

Suffixes: 'ant' or 'ent'; 'ance' or 'ence';
'ancy' or 'ency'? 110
Prefixes: 're', 'dis' or 'mis'? 112
Adding suffixes to words ending 'fer' 113
Synonyms and Antonyms 114
Informal and formal vocabulary 116

Spelling

Letter strings: 'ought' and Letter strings: 'ough' 118
Silent letters 120
'c' or 's'? 121
Adding 'cious' or 'tious' 122
Adding 'tial or 'cial' 123

Adding 'able' or 'ably' and Adding 'ible' or 'ibly' 124
'ei' after 'c' 126
Tricky words 127
Homophones 128
Using dictionaries 130
Using a thesaurus 132

Reading

Identifying main ideas and Identifying key details 134
Summarising main ideas 136
Retrieving and recording information 138
Making comparisons 140
Themes and conventions 142
Fact and opinion 144
Explaining and justifying inferences 146
Predicting what might happen 148
Words in context and Exploring words in context 150
How writers use language 152
Enhancing meaning: figurative language 154
Features of text and Text features
contributing to meaning 156
Asking questions 158

Writing

Planning writing 160
Structuring writing 162
Building cohesion 164
Ellipsis 166
Getting verbs right 167
Précising longer pieces of writing 168
Choosing the right vocabulary and grammar 169
Describing settings and atmosphere 170
Describing characters and using dialogue 172
Editing text 174
Proofreading 176

Year 6 answers 182

About the Planning and Assessment Guides

Scholastic National Curriculum English scheme provides schools and teachers with a flexible scheme of work to meet all of your needs for the English curriculum, allowing you to keep control of what you teach, and when, while saving precious teacher time.

The scheme consists of four components:
- Teacher's *Planning and Assessment Guide*
- Children's *Textbook*
- *100 English Lessons* resource books and CD-ROMs
- Children's *English Practice Book*

The main benefits of the programme include:
- Accessible content geared towards the demands of the National Curriculum.
- Flexibility to fit into the way you already teach using the award-winning *100 English Lessons* teacher's books.
- Detailed support in the *Textbooks* to build secure foundations and deep understanding of key concepts.
- A bank of well-structured exercises in the *Practice Books* linked to clear explanations, which parents can understand and use to help their children.

Using the Planning and Assessment Guide

This book provides guidance on how to introduce topics (including how quickly) and how to support and extend the content in the *Textbook*. It references the accompanying *100 English Lessons* and *Practice Books* so you can use this material to further support learning. Each teaching notes page uses the same heading structure:

- **Prior learning:** details what the children should already know prior to introducing this content.
- **Curriculum objectives and Success criteria:** provides information about which National Curriculum objectives the section covers and the specific success criteria which will come from it.
- **Learn:** relates to the 'Learn' heading in the *Textbook*, but it also goes beyond this and helps you to introduce the learning appropriately.
- **Talk:** provides speaking and listening activities, where relevant.
- **Activities:** gives pointers for those activities in the *Textbook*, as well as giving ideas to extend or support the learning.
- **Write:** provides writing activities to further develop the learning, where relevant.
- *100 English Lessons* and *Practice Book* **links:** these detail related lessons and activities that you can use to enhance and further develop the teaching and learning of the subject area.

Planning and Assessment CD-ROM

The accompanying CD-ROM contains planning and assessment tools, the majority of these have been supplied as a word document so you can edit them to meet your needs. They can be used as effective tools for monitoring performance, identifying areas of weakness and communicating to parents.

Tracking progress
- **English progression overview:** gives an overview of the whole English curriculum across Years 1–6.
- **Teacher tracking:** breaks down an individual year group into three stages of progress 'working towards', 'working at expected level' and 'working at greater depth'.
- **Child progress chart:** 'I can' statements related to the *Textbook*. The children tick to show whether they are 'not sure', are 'getting there' or 'have got' a concept.
- **I can statements:** a cut-out format of the 'I can' statements from the child progress chart.

Planning and reporting templates
For templates – see the template menu on the CD-ROM.
- **Yearly, Termly and Weekly planning:** plan your teaching – templates and completed samples.
- **Termly report:** feed back to parents – templates and completed samples.

Other resources
- **Assessment framework for English:** printable DfE Interim Teacher Assessment frameworks for English
- **Curriculum links:** printable version of the curriculum links found on pages 8–11 of this book.
- **Glossary:** printable version of a child-friendly and age-appropriate English glossary.

Planning with Scholastic English

This series is arrange at a topic level (grammar, spelling, reading, writing) to provide discreet guidance on how to cover the different aspects of the National Curriculum. It is not intended that you would teach this content in a linear fashion, but instead use the content provided to support existing planning or develop new planning incorporating it.

The table on pages 8–11 of this book provides the curriculum objectives with page references to the *Textbook*, *100 English Lessons* and *Practice Book* to assist your planning. There is one omission to this grid, handwriting objectives have not been included due to varied handwriting policies within schools. Handwriting is part of the National Curriculum and provision should be included for this in your planning, both in focussed sessions and throughout general classwork.

About the Textbooks

Using the Textbooks

The *Textbook* and *Planning and Assessment Guide* are arranged thematically and are completely in line with the National Curriculum, allowing teachers and English subject leaders to create long- and medium-term plans best suited to the school's needs. Each section of the *Textbook* presents the 'core' learning for that curriculum area, with the relevant pages in the *Planning and Assessment Guide* providing further advice and links to additional lessons and resources, in particular to *100 English Lessons* and *English Practice Book*.

Textbook structure

Each section has a similar structure.

- **Learn:** examples and facts specific to the objective in question.
- **Tips:** short and simple advice to aid understanding.
- **Activities:** a focused range of questions, with answers provided in the *Planning and Assessment Guide*.

Remember that the *Planning and Assessment Guide* provides advice and links for extending learning and practice in each of these areas.

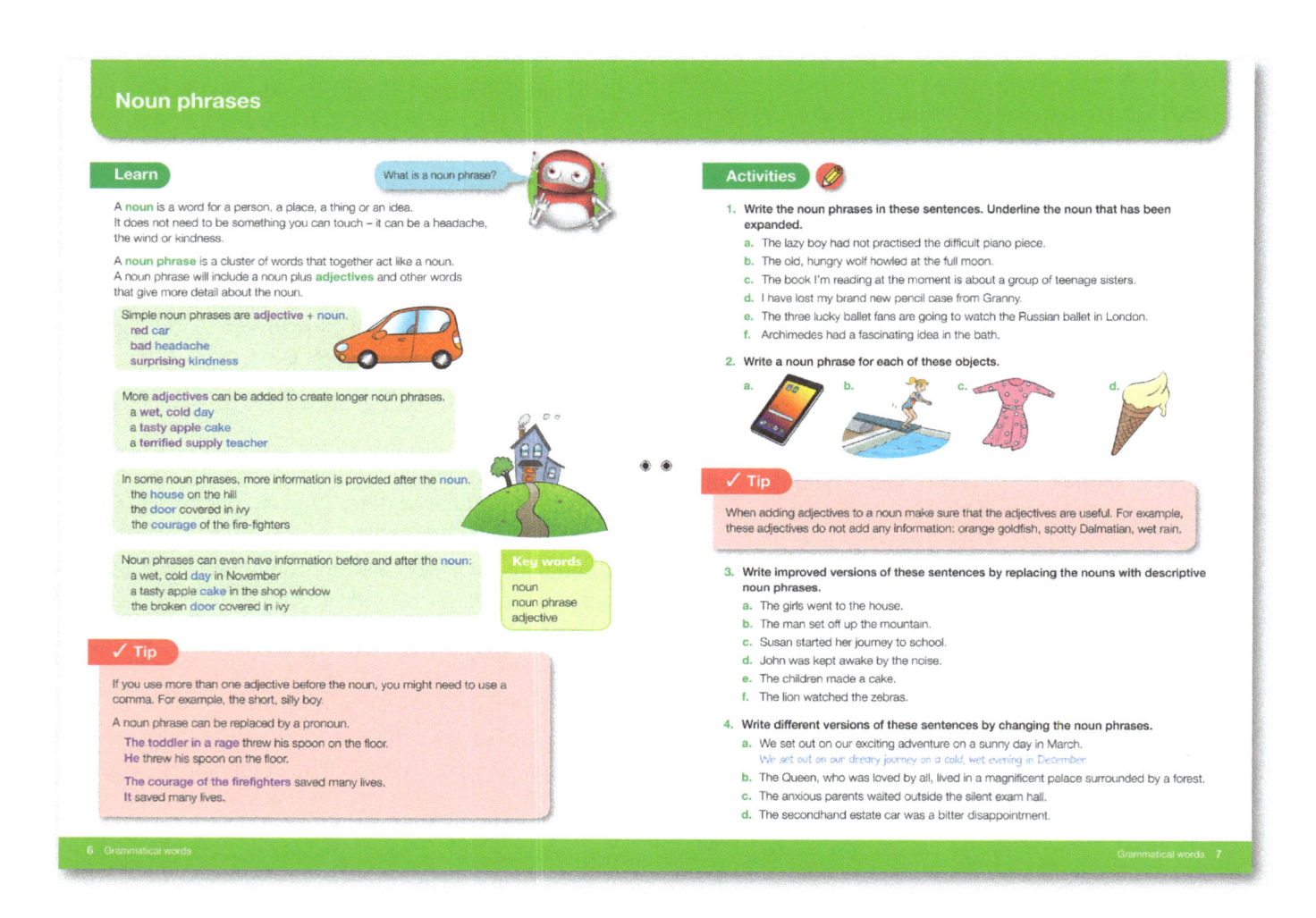

Noun phrases

Learn

What is a noun phrase?

A **noun** is a word for a person, a place, a thing or an idea. It does not need to be something you can touch – it can be a headache, the wind or kindness.

A **noun phrase** is a cluster of words that together act like a noun. A noun phrase will include a noun plus **adjectives** and other words that give more detail about the noun.

Simple noun phrases are adjective + noun.
 red car
 bad headache
 surprising kindness

More adjectives can be added to create longer noun phrases.
 a wet, cold day
 a tasty apple cake
 a terrified supply teacher

In some noun phrases, more information is provided after the noun.
 the house on the hill
 the door covered in ivy
 the courage of the fire-fighters

Noun phrases can even have information before and after the noun:
 a wet, cold day in November
 a tasty apple cake in the shop window
 the broken door covered in ivy

Key words
noun
noun phrase
adjective

✓ Tip

If you use more than one adjective before the noun, you might need to use a comma. For example, the short, silly boy.

A noun phrase can be replaced by a pronoun.
 The toddler in a rage threw his spoon on the floor.
 He threw his spoon on the floor.

 The courage of the firefighters saved many lives.
 It saved many lives.

Activities

1. Write the noun phrases in these sentences. Underline the noun that has been expanded.
   a. The lazy boy had not practised the difficult piano piece.
   b. The old, hungry wolf howled at the full moon.
   c. The book I'm reading at the moment is about a group of teenage sisters.
   d. I have lost my brand new pencil case from Granny.
   e. The three lucky ballet fans are going to watch the Russian ballet in London.
   f. Archimedes had a fascinating idea in the bath.

2. Write a noun phrase for each of these objects.
   a.   b.   c.   d.

✓ Tip

When adding adjectives to a noun make sure that the adjectives are useful. For example, these adjectives do not add any information: orange goldfish, spotty Dalmatian, wet rain.

3. Write improved versions of these sentences by replacing the nouns with descriptive noun phrases.
   a. The girls went to the house.
   b. The man set off up the mountain.
   c. Susan started her journey to school.
   d. John was kept awake by the noise.
   e. The children made a cake.
   f. The lion watched the zebras.

4. Write different versions of these sentences by changing the noun phrases.
   a. We set out on our exciting adventure on a sunny day in March.
      We set out on our dreary journey on a cold, wet evening in December.
   b. The Queen, who was loved by all, lived in a magnificent palace surrounded by a forest.
   c. The anxious parents waited outside the silent exam hall.
   d. The secondhand estate car was a bitter disappointment.

---

6 Planning and Assessment Guide

Tracking progress

Assessment is always an ongoing process – formative assessments provide feedback to teacher and child for next steps; summative assessment provides snapshots of a child's current competence.

There is a self-assessment chart for children on the CD-ROM (Child progress chart). This is intended as a method of engaging children in considering their own achievement; it might also be referenced by teachers in making their own judgements. Each 'I can' statement is a generalisation for each section in the Textbook. These statements are also provided in a cut-out and stick format.

The CD-ROM also provides a progression overview document – summarising the progress between year groups and a teacher tracking grid that allows you to track more detailed progress within a year group. The teacher tracking grid breaks each curriculum objective down into working towards the expected standard, working at the expected standard or working with greater depth. Each of these terms is explained below.

Working towards the expected standard

At this stage, children are able to access the objective at a simple level, or with some kind of support, whether from an adult, a peer or via some form of supportive resource. Children requiring support to complete work may:

- read a some texts for different purposes and demonstrate some understanding of these with support.
- write texts with emerging skills.
- can write for a purpose and audience only when scaffolding is provided.
- have difficulty correcting mistakes.

Working at the expected standard

Children working at the expected level on an English objective will be able to fulfil the essence of the objective independently. Indications that children are working at the expected standard for a particular objective include:

- read and demonstrate understanding of a wide range of age-appropriate texts for a range of purposes.
- write good-quality texts.
- demonstrate some understanding of purpose and audience in their writing.
- correct their own mistakes in work marked by others.

Working at greater depth

This category suggests that children have mastered the objective involved. They can demonstrate the skills used independently in a range of context. Indicators that children are working at greater depth include:

- read and demonstrate understanding of more demanding texts for a range of purposes.
- write longer, better-quality texts.
- demonstrate an understanding of purpose and audience when writing.
- spot errors and self-correct them.

DFE interim guidance (2015) on English assessment is available on the CD-ROM.

Scholastic English and Mastery

There are many definitions of 'mastery' in English. As well as judging how much a child has learned, it is important to assess how well they apply their learning. Children's English knowledge should be applied across all National Curriculum areas, this helps to give purpose to the skills they are learning and help deepen understanding. The level to which they can do this is one definition of mastery.

Scholastic National Curriculum English offers many opportunities for children to demonstrate using the skills they have learned. The 100 English Lessons content provides content based around children's books to develop children's learning. To deepen or embed these skills the English Practice Books and Textbooks offer a range of well-structured exercises. The range of opportunities within the programme to embed or apply English skills therefore should provide teachers with sufficient evidence to track how secure English concepts are and whether they have truly been mastered by each child.

An individual report template has been provided on the CD-ROM to feed back to parents how well their child can apply their skills that they have learned. This might be done termly or at other times when children have attained a secure level of mastery in a particular area.

Curriculum objectives	Year 5 Textbook	100 English Lessons Year 5	Year 5 Practice Book
Word recognition			
To apply their growing knowledge of root words, prefixes and suffixes (morphology and etymology), as listed in the Spelling appendix, both to read aloud and to understand the meaning of new words that they meet.	Pages: 22, 23	Pages: 21, 34, 61, 62, 90, 117	
Reading comprehension			
To continue to read and discuss an increasingly wide range of fiction, poetry, plays, non-fiction and reference books or textbooks.	Pages: 43	Pages: 31, 34, 35, 36, 38, 51, 61, 66, 67, 98,99, 115, 116, 130, 131, 132, 150, 156, 188, 189, 191, 192, 194, 195	Note: the entire Comprehension section could be used to support various comprehension objectives
To read books that are structured in different ways and reading for a range of purposes.	Pages: 46–47	Pages: 28, 125, 163, 180	
To increase their familiarity with a wide range of books, including myths, legends and traditional stories, modern fiction, fiction from our literary heritage, and books from other cultures and traditions.	Pages: 48–49	Pages: 19, 20, 28, 38, 89, 92, 93, 150, 159, 160	
To recommend books that they have read to their peers, giving reasons for their choices.	Pages: 42	Pages: 94	
To identify and discuss themes and conventions in and across a wide range of writing.	Pages: 48–49	Pages: 19, 53, 57, 87, 89, 128, 129, 159, 160, 162, 194, 195	
To make comparisons within and across books.	Pages: 46–47	Pages: 28, 87, 116, 125, 126, 160	
To learn a wider range of poetry by heart.	Pages: 58–59	Pages: 35, 99, 131, 194	
To prepare poems and plays to read aloud and to perform, showing understanding through intonation, tone and volume so that the meaning is clear to an audience.	Pages: 58–59, 74–75	Pages: 36, 68, 88, 93, 99, 131	
To check that the book makes sense to them, discussing their understanding and exploring the meaning of words in context.	Pages: 54, 55	Pages: 34, 52, 185, 186, 188, 189	
To ask questions to improve their understanding.	Pages: 62, 63	Pages: 22, 51, 53, 95, 96, 163, 180, 183, 188, 189	Pages: 48
To draw inferences such as inferring characters' feelings, thoughts and motives from their actions, and justifying inferences with evidence.	Pages: 52–53	Pages: 20, 51, 58, 61, 62, 126	Pages: 86–102
To predict what might happen from details stated and implied.	Pages: 43	Pages: 116, 126, 188	
To summarise the main ideas drawn from more than one paragraph, identifying key details that support the main ideas.	Pages: 40, 41, 42	Pages: 20, 63, 70, 84, 102, 128, 179, 180, 182, 183, 191	
To identify how language, structure and presentation contribute to meaning.	Pages: 60, 61	Pages: 26, 27, 55, 61, 157, 162, 163	
To discuss and evaluate how authors use language, including figurative language, considering the impact on the reader.	Pages: 56–57, 58–59	Pages: 20, 25, 26, 38, 66, 67, 99, 122, 127, 153, 158, 162, 163, 166, 192, 195	Pages: 50, 102–103
To distinguish between statements of fact and opinion.	Pages: 50–51	Pages: 22, 23, 119, 121, 122, 153, 154, 179, 180, 191, 198	
To retrieve, record and present information from non-fiction.	Pages: 44–45	Pages: 22, 24, 54, 55, 83, 84, 85, 95, 96, 97, 103, 119, 147, 154, 163, 180, 183, 188, 189	Pages: 104–105
To participate in discussions about books that are read to them and those they can read for themselves, building on their own and others' ideas and challenging views courteously.	Pages: 50–51	Pages: 28, 29, 31, 57, 58, 92, 117, 118, 120, 121, 124, 125, 126, 156, 159	
To explain and discuss their understanding of what they have read, including through formal presentations and debates, maintaining a focus on the topic and using notes where necessary.	Pages: 62, 63	Pages: 52, 84, 85, 94, 119, 120, 121, 151, 189, 192, 193	
To provide reasoned justifications for their views.	Pages: 62, 63	Pages: 20, 57, 58, 59,	
Transcription – Spelling			
To use further prefixes and suffixes and understand the guidance for adding them.	Pages: 22, 23, 24, 25, 26, 27, 28	Pages: 26, 30, 117, 133, 149, 196, 197	Pages: 14–15, 16–17, 18–19, 20–21, 65–66, 67, 68
To spell some words with 'silent' letters.	Pages: 31	Pages: 21, 184	Pages: 28–29
To continue to distinguish between homophones and other words which are often confused.	Pages: 35	Pages: 32, 37, 181	Pages: 33, 34, 35, 36, 37, 38, 39, 40, 41, 42, 43, 44, 45
To use knowledge of morphology and etymology in spelling and understand that the spelling of some words needs to be learned specifically, as listed in the Spelling appendix.	Pages: 36–37	Pages: 14, 32, 60, 62, 69, 91, 101, 158, 161, 164, 165, 193, 196	
To use dictionaries to check the spelling and meaning of words.	Pages: 38–39	Pages: 32, 51, 90, 162, 183, 195, 196	
To use the first three or four letters of a word to check spelling, meaning or both of these in a dictionary.	Pages: 38–39	Pages: 32, 51, 90, 161, 162, 195	
To spell endings which sound like /shus/ spelled 'cious' or 'tious'. (Spelling appendix)	Pages: 32	Pages: 21, 158	Pages: 6–7
To spell endings which sound like /shul/. (Spelling appendix)	Pages: 33		Pages: 8–9
To spell words ending in 'ant', 'ance'/'ancy', 'ent', 'ence'/'ency'. (Spelling appendix)	Pages: 34	Pages: 30, 193	Pages: 10–11, 12–13

8 Planning and Assessment Guide

Curriculum objectives	Year 5 Textbook	100 English Lessons Year 5	Year 5 Practice Book
To spell words ending in 'able' and 'ible'. (Spelling appendix)	Pages: 26, 27	Pages: 26	Pages: 14–15, 16–17
To spell words ending in 'ably' and 'ibly'. (Spelling appendix)	Pages: 26, 27	Pages: 26	Pages: 14–15, 16–17
To adding suffixes beginning with vowel letters to words ending in 'fer'. (Spelling appendix)	Pages: 28		Pages: 18–19
To spell words with the /ee/ sound spelled 'ei' after 'c'. (Spelling appendix)	Pages: 29	Pages: 12, 62, 69	Pages: 22–23
To spell words containing the letter string 'ough'. (Spelling appendix)	Pages: 30	Pages: 21, 101, 184	Pages: 24–25, 26–27
Composition			
To identify the audience for and purpose of the writing, selecting the appropriate form and using other similar writing as models for their own.	Pages: 64–65	Pages: 65, 97, 100, 119, 120, 154, 196	Pages: 106–107, 108–109, 112–113, 114–115, 121, 126, 127
To note and develop initial ideas, drawing on reading and research where necessary.	Pages: 64–65	Pages: 24, 29, 33, 54, 55, 97, 119, 120, 123, 164, 181, 183, 184, 185, 186, 189, 190, 196	Pages: 106–107, 108–109, 112–113, 114–115, 121, 126, 127
In writing narratives, to considering how authors have developed characters and settings in what they have read, listened to or seen performed.	Pages: 72–73	Pages: 30, 64, 123, 128, 129, 185, 186	Pages: 110–111, 112–113
To select appropriate grammar and vocabulary, understanding how such choices can change and enhance meaning.	Pages: 56–57, 71	Pages: 27, 33, 61, 68, 132, 135, 155, 164, 167, 184, 187, 193, 199	Pages: 46
In narratives, to describe settings, characters and atmosphere and integrate dialogue to convey character and advance the action.	Pages: 72–73, 74–75	Pages: 20, 27, 58, 59, 88, 160, 161, 187	Pages: 110–111, 112–113, 114–115, 116–117
To précis longer passages	Pages: 80	Pages: 64, 119, 120, 134, 148, 149, 150, 160, 180	
To use a wide range of devices to build cohesion within and across paragraphs.	Pages: 68–69	Pages: 27, 33, 85, 88, 155, 161, 181, 184, 187, 199	Pages: 69–70, 71, 72
To use further organisational and presentational devices to structure text and to guide the reader.	Pages: 66	Pages: 24, 55, 71, 148, 149, 181, 190	
To assess the effectiveness of their own and others' writing.	Pages: 76–77	Pages: 27, 64, 97, 100, 167, 181, 184, 190, 196	Pages: 126, 127
To propose changes to vocabulary, grammar and punctuation to enhance effects and clarify meaning.	Pages: 76–77	Pages: 64, 90, 91, 97, 132, 196	Pages: 126, 127
To ensure the consistent and correct use of tense throughout a piece of writing.	Pages: 67	Pages: 129, 190	Pages: 123–125
To ensure correct subject and verb agreement when using singular and plural, distinguishing between the language of speech and writing and choosing the appropriate register.	Pages: 67	Pages: 53, 59, 85, 190, 197	Pages: 123–125
To proofread for spelling and punctuation errors.	Pages: 78–79	Pages: 64, 65, 129, 135, 187, 190	
To perform their own compositions, using appropriate intonation, volume, and movement so that meaning is clear.	Pages: 58–59	Pages: 29, 33, 36, 85, 100, 157, 189	
Vocabulary, grammar and punctuation			
To use the perfect form of verbs to mark relationships of time and cause.	Pages: 8–9	Pages: 20	Pages: 56, 57
To use expanded noun phrases to convey complicated information concisely.	Pages: 6–7	Pages: 126, 133	Pages: 51, 52, 53, 54, 55
To use modal verbs or adverbs to indicate degrees of possibility.	Pages: 10, 11	Pages: 23, 24, 155, 184	Pages: 58–60
To use relative clauses beginning with 'who', 'which', 'where', 'when', 'whose', 'that' or with an implied relative pronoun.	Pages: 12–13	Pages: 56, 59, 69, 88, 96	Pages: 61–62, 63–64
To use commas to clarify meaning or avoid ambiguity in writing.	Pages: 14–15	Pages: 56, 59, 88, 90	Pages: 75–76, 77, 78
To use hyphens to avoid ambiguity.	Pages: 24–25	Pages: 33, 37	Pages: 20–21, 83
To use brackets, dashes or commas to indicate parenthesis.	Pages: 16–17	Pages: 91, 101, 123	Pages: 79–80, 81
To use a colon to introduce a list.	Pages: 20	Pages: 148, 149, 160, 191	Pages: 82
To punctuate bullet points consistently.	Pages: 21	Pages: 55, 148, 149, 165, 181	Pages: 84–85, 108–109
To convert nouns or adjectives into verbs using suffixes (for example, 'ate', 'ise', 'ify'). (Grammar appendix)	Pages: 24, 25	Pages: 60	Pages: 65–66
To use verb prefixes (for example, 'dis', 'de', 'mis', 'over' and 're'). (Grammar appendix)	Pages: 22, 23	Pages: 13, 117, 133	Pages: 20–21, 67, 68
To link ideas across paragraphs using adverbials of time, place and number or tense choices. (Grammar appendix)	Pages: 70	Pages: 23	Pages: 58–60, 69–70

Curriculum objectives	Year 6 Textbook	100 English Lessons Year 6	Year 6 Practice Book
Word recognition			
To apply their growing knowledge of root words, prefixes and suffixes (morphology and etymology), as listed in the Spelling appendix, both to read aloud and to understand the meaning of new words that they meet.	Pages: 30	Pages: 54, 60, 61, 84, 85, 101	Pages: 20–21, 68–69
Reading comprehension			
To continue to read and discuss an increasingly wide range of fiction, poetry, plays, non-fiction and reference books or textbooks.	Pages: 66–67	Pages: 19, 20, 21, 28, 34, 35, 36, 63, 83, 84, 85, 98, 99, 130, 134, 159, 160, 194	Note: the entire Comprehension section could be used to support various comprehension objectives
To read books that are structured in different ways and reading for a range of purposes.	Pages: 58–59	Pages: 93, 127, 128, 159	
To increase their familiarity with a wide range of books, including myths, legends and traditional stories, modern fiction, fiction from our literary heritage, and books from other cultures and traditions.	Pages: 60–61	Pages: 19, 21, 51, 52, 70, 83, 84, 85, 102, 118, 119, 159, 179, 180	
To recommend books that they have read to their peers, giving reasons for their choices.	Pages: 54–55	Pages: 91, 117	
To identify and discuss themes and conventions in and across a wide range of writing.	Pages: 60–61	Pages: 27, 31, 32, 35, 36, 83, 84, 85, 87, 88, 89, 90, 118, 119, 120, 147, 150, 151, 158, 162, 163, 164, 166, 189, 195	
To make comparisons within and across books.	Pages: 58–59	Pages: 31, 87, 88, 118, 119, 120, 124, 125, 147, 150, 151	
To learn a wider range of poetry by heart.	Pages: 72–73	Pages: 35, 61, 98, 99, 163, 164, 195	
To prepare poems and plays to read aloud and to perform, showing understanding through intonation, tone and volume so that the meaning is clear to an audience.	Pages: 72–73	Pages: 35, 36, 61, 62, 63, 64, 65, 98, 99, 131, 134, 162, 163, 164, 194, 196	
To check that the book makes sense to them, discussing their understanding and exploring the meaning of words in context.	Pages: 68, 69	Pages: 54, 55, 60, 61, 62, 70, 84, 148, 182	
To ask questions to improve their understanding.	Pages: 76–77	Pages: 51, 52, 70, 89, 90, 91, 92, 93, 125, 148, 157, 158, 185, 189	
To draw inferences such as inferring characters' feelings, thoughts and motives from their actions, and justifying inferences with evidence.	Pages: 64–65	Pages: 19, 20, 21, 25, 26, 27, 38, 51, 55, 64, 70, 84, 85, 124, 125, 147, 148, 159, 160, 166, 179, 180, 198	
To predict what might happen from details stated and implied.	Pages: 66–67	Pages: 19, 83, 119, 147, 148, 179	
To summarise the main ideas drawn from more than one paragraph, identifying key details that support the main ideas.	Pages: 52, 53, 54–55	Pages: 25, 26, 27, 54, 55, 56, 89, 90, 147, 148, 150, 156, 157, 160, 166, 188	Pages: 100–101, 118–119
To identify how language, structure and presentation contribute to meaning.	Pages: 74, 75	Pages: 34, 35, 36, 52, 70, 86, 88, 102, 148, 163	
To discuss and evaluate how authors use language, including figurative language, considering the impact on the reader.	Pages: 70–71, 72–73	Pages: 20, 21, 34, 35, 38, 92, 98, 99, 102, 126, 130, 131, 134, 180, 182, 194, 198	
To distinguish between statements of fact and opinion.	Pages: 62–63	Pages: 22, 122, 183, 191	
To retrieve, record and present information from non-fiction.	Pages: 56–57	Pages: 22, 32, 66, 96, 97, 115, 121, 122, 153, 154, 155, 183, 185, 186, 189, 191, 192, 193	Pages: 120
To participate in discussions about books that are read to them and those they can read for themselves, building on their own and others' ideas and challenging views courteously.	Pages: 62–63	Pages: 21, 25, 26, 27, 30, 38, 51, 118, 119, 124, 125, 126, 128, 129, 156, 157, 182, 183, 186, 189, 198	
To explain and discuss their understanding of what they have read, including through formal presentations and debates, maintaining a focus on the topic and using notes where necessary.	Pages: 76–77	Pages: 28, 30, 89, 90, 91, 92, 124, 126, 128, 158, 179, 180, 185, 186, 193	
To provide reasoned justifications for their views.	Pages: 76–77	Pages: 28, 30, 38, 90, 127, 128, 129, 157, 158, 185, 189, 198	
Transcription – Spelling			
To use further prefixes and suffixes and understand the guidance for adding them.	Pages: 28–29, 30	Pages: 25, 29, 159	Pages: 10–13, 20–21, 68–69
To spell some words with 'silent' letters.	Pages: 38	Pages: 14, 184, 187, 197	Pages: 28–29
To continue to distinguish between homophones and other words which are often confused.	Pages: 46–47	Pages: 11, 57, 58, 59, 69	Pages: 33–35, 36–38, 39–41, 42–44, 45
To use knowledge of morphology and etymology in spelling and understand that the spelling of some words needs to be learned specifically, as listed in the Spelling appendix.	Pages: 39, 45	Pages: 22, 25, 27, 37, 101, 125, 133, 164, 165, 183, 195	Pages: 30–32
To use dictionaries to check the spelling and meaning of words.	Pages: 48–49	Pages: 24, 33, 36, 54, 55, 60, 61, 69, 84, 101, 117, 128, 182, 183, 187	
To use the first three or four letters of a word to check spelling, meaning or both of these in a dictionary.	Pages: 48–49	Pages: 32, 37, 60, 84, 128	
To use a thesaurus.	Pages: 50–51	Pages: 33, 36, 85, 100, 190, 196	Pages: 46–47
To spell endings which sound like /shus/ spelled 'cious' or 'tious'. (Spelling appendix)	Pages: 40	Pages: 11, 22	Pages: 6–7
To spell endings which sound like /shul/. (Spelling appendix)	Pages: 41	Pages: 11, 37	Pages: 8–9
To spell words ending in 'ant', 'ance'/'ancy', 'ent', 'ence'/'ency'. (Spelling appendix)	Pages: 28–29	Pages: 11	Pages: 10–13

Curriculum objectives	Year 6 Textbook	100 English Lessons Year 6	Year 6 Practice Book
To spell words ending in 'able' and 'ible'. To spell words ending in 'ably' and 'ibly'. (Spelling appendix)	Pages: 42	Pages: 11, 29, 165	Pages: 14–17
To adding suffixes beginning with vowel letters to words ending in 'fer'. (Spelling appendix)	Pages: 31		Pages: 18–19
To spell words with the /ee/ sound spelled 'ei' after 'c'. (Spelling appendix)	Pages: 44		Pages: 22–23
To spell words containing the letter-string 'ough'. (Spelling appendix)	Pages: 36, 37	Pages: 120, 133, 183	Pages: 24–27
Composition			
To identify the audience for and purpose of the writing, selecting the appropriate form and using other similar writing as models for their own.	Pages: 78–79	Pages: 23, 24, 53, 66, 67, 68, 71, 94, 100, 116, 120, 127, 129, 184, 190, 196	Pages: 106, 126–127
To note and develop initial ideas, drawing on reading and research where necessary.	Pages: 78–79	Pages: 23, 24, 28, 29, 95, 97, 99, 126, 129, 160, 161, 183, 190, 196	Pages: 106, 126–127
In writing narratives, to consider how authors have developed characters and settings in what they have read, listened to or seen performed.	Pages: 88–89	Pages: 32, 33, 39, 59, 71, 129, 161, 167, 181, 199	Pages: 110–111, 112–113
To select appropriate grammar and vocabulary, understanding how such choices can change and enhance meaning.	Pages: 87	Pages: 27, 32, 33, 36, 53, 56, 58, 59, 61, 62, 71, 86, 88, 93, 94, 103, 132, 184, 187, 188, 190	
In narratives, to describe settings, characters and atmosphere and integrate dialogue to convey character and advance the action.	Pages: 88–89, 90–91	Pages: 31, 32, 33, 39, 59, 103, 151, 152, 167, 190, 199	Pages: 110–111, 112–113, 114–115, 116–117
To précis longer passages.	Pages: 86	Pages: 65, 66, 122, 154, 155, 160	
To use a wide range of devices to build cohesion within and across paragraphs.	Pages: 82–83	Pages: 29, 30, 33, 39, 96, 97, 103, 116, 123, 135, 154, 155, 187, 190, 193	Pages: 70–74, 118–119
To use further organisational and presentational devices to structure text and to guide the reader.	Pages: 80–81	Pages: 23, 24, 87, 116, 123, 135, 149	Pages: 120, 121–122
To assess the effectiveness of their own and others' writing.	Pages: 92–93	Pages: 23, 24, 27, 31, 39, 59, 71, 96, 97, 100, 116, 123, 135, 161, 184, 187, 190	
To propose changes to vocabulary, grammar and punctuation to enhance effects and clarify meaning.	Pages: 92–93	Pages: 33, 59, 68, 71, 96, 97, 117, 184	
To ensure the consistent and correct use of tense throughout a piece of writing.	Pages: 85	Pages: 96, 97, 183, 184	Pages: 123–125
To ensure correct subject and verb agreement when using singular and plural, distinguishing between the language of speech and writing and choosing the appropriate register.	Pages: 85	Pages: 96, 97, 161, 167, 199	Pages: 123–125
To proofread for spelling and punctuation errors.	Pages: 94–95	Pages: 33, 96, 97, 117, 133, 184, 190, 193	
To perform their own compositions, using appropriate intonation, volume, and movement so that meaning is clear.	Pages: 72–73	Pages: 36, 100	
Vocabulary, grammar and punctuation			
To recognise vocabulary and structures that are appropriate for formal speech and writing, including subjunctive forms.	Pages: 16–17	Pages: 56, 88, 187, 192	Pages: 58–59
To use passive verbs to affect the presentation of information in a sentence.	Pages: 14–15	Pages: 56, 69, 88, 93, 94, 119, 149, 154, 155, 184, 187, 192	Pages: 62–63
To use the perfect form of verbs to mark relationships of time and cause.	Pages: 8	Pages: 27, 33	Pages: 56–57
To use expanded noun phrases to convey complicated information concisely.	Pages: 6–7	Pages: 120, 133, 151, 152, 154, 167, 184	Pages: 53–55
To use modal verbs or adverbs to indicate degrees of possibility.	Pages: 10, 11	Pages: 155, 184, 187	Pages: 60–61
To use relative clauses beginning with 'who', 'which', 'where', 'when', 'whose', 'that' or with an implied relative pronoun.	Pages: 9	Pages: 154, 155, 165	Pages: 64–65
To use commas to clarify meaning or avoid ambiguity in writing.	Pages: 18	Pages: 123, 154, 192	Pages: 75–76
To use hyphens to avoid ambiguity.	Pages: 20	Pages: 123, 154, 181, 197	Pages: 20–21, 83
To use brackets, dashes or commas to indicate parenthesis.	Pages: 26–27	Pages: 63, 65, 71, 94, 103, 123, 154, 192	Pages: 79–80
To use semi-colons, colons or dashes to mark boundaries between independent clauses.	Pages: 24–25	Pages: 52, 63, 65, 71, 86, 87, 101, 103, 119, 123, 154, 180	Pages: 77–78
To use a colon to introduce a list.	Pages: 22–23	Pages: 53, 67, 87, 154	Pages: 81–82
To punctuate bullet points consistently.	Pages: 21	Pages: 23, 24, 37, 87, 116, 123, 188, 192	Pages: 84–85
To use and understand the grammar in English Appendix 2 accurately and appropriately when discussing their writing and reading.	Pages: 12–13	Pages: 29, 30, 33, 56, 86, 93, 181, 188, 190, 195, 196	Pages: 123–125
To know the difference between structures typical of informal speech and structures appropriate for formal speech and writing. (Grammar appendix)	Pages: 16–17, 19, 34–35	Pages: 51–53, 54–56, 88, 102–103, 127–129, 148, 181, 182–184, 188–190	Pages: 58–59, 50, 51, 52
To understand how words are related by meaning as synonyms and antonyms. (Grammar appendix)	Pages: 32, 33	Pages: 14, 33, 188–190, 194–196	Pages: 48–49
To link ideas across paragraphs using adverbials of time (for example, later), place (for example, nearby) and number (for example, secondly) or tense choices (for example, he had seen her before). (Grammar appendix)	Pages: 82–83, 84		Pages: 70–74, 118–119

Noun phrases

Prior learning

- Understand and identify nouns, pronouns, adjectives and prepositions.
- Know that a phrase is a group of words.

Learn

- Remind the children that many nouns can be touched, but others cannot. Walk around the classroom touching and naming some nouns – wall, floor, window.
- Explain that an abstract noun is something that you cannot touch, such as a headache or kindness. Ask them to offer examples, testing them out inside their heads by seeing if 'a', 'an' or 'the' would go comfortably in front of the word. Prompt them by giving clues. For instance, tell them that many of them will have different emotions and feelings which they could give a name to, such as happiness, excitement or thoughtfulness.
- Recall what a noun phrase is – a noun with words around it (often adjectives) that describe it.
- Ask the children, in pairs or threes, to look around the classroom identifying nouns and adding a simple adjective in front. Encourage them to think of colour, shape and texture.
- Turn this into a game of word tennis between two halves of the class where you give a few seconds' time limit for a hand to go up to return the 'ball'.

Curriculum objectives

- To use expanded noun phrases to convey complicated information concisely.

Success criteria

- I can identify a noun phrase in a given sentence.
- I can write my own noun phrase.

Noun phrases

Learn

What is a noun phrase?

A **noun** is a word for a person, a place, a thing or an idea. It does not need to be something you can touch – it can be a headache, the wind or kindness.

A **noun phrase** is a cluster of words that together act like a noun. A noun phrase will include a noun plus **adjectives** and other words that give more detail about the noun.

Simple noun phrases are **adjective** + **noun**.
  red car
  bad headache
  surprising kindness

More **adjectives** can be added to create longer noun phrases.
  a wet, cold day
  a tasty apple cake
  a terrified supply teacher

In some noun phrases, more information is provided after the **noun**.
  the house on the hill
  the door covered in ivy
  the courage of the fire-fighters

Noun phrases can even have information before and after the **noun**:
  a wet, cold day in November
  a tasty apple cake in the shop window
  the broken door covered in ivy

Key words
noun
noun phrase
adjective

✓ Tip

If you use more than one adjective before the noun, you might need to use a comma. For example, the short, silly boy.

A noun phrase can be replaced by a pronoun.
  The toddler in a rage threw his spoon on the floor.
  He threw his spoon on the floor.

  The courage of the firefighters saved many lives.
  It saved many lives.

- Increase the difficulty by asking for longer noun phrases with multiple adjectives, prepositional phrases and altering where the additional information about the noun comes in the sentence (see the textbook examples).
- Starter activity 7 from *100 English Lessons Year 5* or *100 English Lessons Year 5, Spring 2, Week 4, Lesson 5* could be used to reinforce these skills further.

Activities

- Use the activities in the textbook and on pages 51–55 of the *Year 5 Practice Book* to consolidate understanding.
- Asking the children to create their own sentences containing two expanded noun phrases. Suggest looking around the classroom for ideas or using their imagination to create a sentence that might be the opening or part of a story.
- Ask the children to write a crazy story that contains as many of their answers to the textbook activities as possible. Encourage them to add new noun phrases and to have a variety of different structures. For instance, the story could begin, 'They were told never to go to the creepy house, but the two unfortunate girls did go to that mysterious mansion, setting out on their dreary journey on a cold, wet evening in December'. The idea is to pack the story with expanded noun phrases, so it might end up being quite a strange story indeed!

Activities

1. Write the noun phrases in these sentences. Underline the noun that has been expanded.
    a. The lazy boy had not practised the difficult piano piece.
    b. The old, hungry wolf howled at the full moon.
    c. The book I'm reading at the moment is about a group of teenage sisters.
    d. I have lost my brand new pencil case from Granny.
    e. The three lucky ballet fans are going to watch the Russian ballet in London.
    f. Archimedes had a fascinating idea in the bath.

2. Write a noun phrase for each of these objects.
    a.   b.   c.   d.

✓ Tip

When adding adjectives to a noun make sure that the adjectives are useful. For example, these adjectives do not add any information: orange goldfish, spotty Dalmatian, wet rain.

3. Write improved versions of these sentences by replacing the nouns with descriptive noun phrases.
    a. The girls went to the house.
    b. The man set off up the mountain.
    c. Susan started her journey to school.
    d. John was kept awake by the noise.
    e. The children made a cake.
    f. The lion watched the zebras.

4. Write different versions of these sentences by changing the noun phrases.
    a. We set out on our exciting adventure on a sunny day in March.
    We set out on our dreary journey on a cold, wet evening in December.
    b. The Queen, who was loved by all, lived in a magnificent palace surrounded by a forest.
    c. The anxious parents waited outside the silent exam hall.
    d. The secondhand estate car was a bitter disappointment.

100 English Lessons Year 5 links:

- Starter activity 7 (page 13): All in a noun phrase
- Spring 2, Week 4 (page 126): Lesson 5, Noun phrases
- Spring 2, Assess and review (page 133): Noun phrases

Year 5 Practice Book links:

- (page 51): Introducing expanded noun phrases
- (page 52): More expanded noun phrases
- (page 53): Expand it
- (page 54): Info-packed phrases
- (page 55): Slick descriptions

Perfect form of verbs

Prior learning

- Understand the difference between past tense and present tense.
- Use verbs in both the present and past tenses.
- Know the present perfect form.

Learn

- Check that the children understand the difference between the past and present tenses. Find two passages from novel openings where one is written in the present tense and one in the past. Read them aloud first to see if they can spot any differences. Read again, but slowly, writing out four or five verbs on the whiteboard as you get to them.
- Remind the children about the present perfect form of verbs – where the past tense of the verb is used with 'have' or has' in order to show that this action affects the situation now.
- Ask for two confident volunteers to come to the front for an improvised conversation. Give one of them the opening line 'I have decided to paint the bedroom', asking the other to reply and for the pair of them to then carry on the conversation for a few more moments. It may end up going something like:
  - A: I have decided to paint the bedroom.
  - B: Have you?
  - A: Yes.
  - B: What colour?
  - A: Red.
  - B: When are you getting started?
- Now ask the children whether or not the bedroom has actually been painted yet. Try the other examples, again with volunteers.
- Explain that we can also use the past perfect form where we use 'had' and the past tense of the verb to show something has happened, but it's not important when. Repeat the conversation activity with examples to show the difference.

Curriculum objectives

- To use the perfect form of verbs to mark relationships of time and cause.

Success criteria

- I can identify and use the present perfect and the past perfect.

Perfect form of verbs

Learn

What is the perfect form of verbs?

Present perfect

We can use the past tense with 'have/has' to show that something has happened, but it doesn't really matter when it happened. The important information is that it has happened and this affects the situation now.

> I have decided to paint the bedroom.

(I made a decision in the past and now I am going to paint the bedroom.)

> Josh has been given a new phone.

(Josh was given a phone. Now he has a phone.)

> Stephanie has always wanted to go to Peru.

(Stephanie wanted to go to Peru in the past and still wants to go.)

> It has stopped raining.

(The rain stopped and now it is not raining.)

Past perfect

We can use the past tense with 'had' to show that something happened (but it's not important when it happened) and this affected something after that but still in the past.

> I had decided to paint the bedroom.

(I made the decision and then I was going to paint the bedroom. For some reason this is no longer the case – perhaps I have painted the bedroom or decided not to after all.)

> Josh had been given a new phone.

(Josh was given a new phone. He then had a new phone at the point in question – perhaps that meant he was able to phone to say he was running late, or perhaps it meant he didn't get given something else.)

> It had stopped raining.

(The rain stopped. It was then not raining. This whole event has now past.)

Key words

present perfect
past perfect

✓ **Tip**

Present perfect verbs can also be about things that haven't happened.

Charlie has not done his homework. Benji and Paul have not been allowed to go on the school trip.

8 Grammatical words

Talk

- Make up some fun present or past perfect opening sentences for improvised dialogue. Let the children experiment with improvising a dialogue in pairs. Tell them there is no need to write it down. Ask for volunteers to recreate their conversations in front of the class. This can be done from their seats or by coming out to the front.

Activities

- Use the activities in the textbook and on pages 56–57 of the *Year 5 Practice Book* to consolidate understanding.
- Challenge the children to pick one of their answers for activity 3 from the textbook and continue it as a piece of writing which uses more present perfect verbs. For instance, 'The sun has appeared over the fence and the rain has stopped. The flowers have opened and the leaves of grass have raised their heads…'
- Following activity 4, ask the children to choose one of their sentences as the beginning of a story and to try to follow on with a range of past perfect verbs. For instance, 'The balloon had flown all the way to Australia. It had started in a garden in England. The wind had howled and the rain had drizzled on the day it had set off…'

Activities

1. Which of these sentences use the present perfect? Write down the sentences.
   a. Bonny has not practised enough for her violin exam.
   b. Sasha has trained very hard for the race.
   c. Matthew has curly hair.
   d. We have brought our wellie boots just in case.
   e. Please can you give out the books?
   f. I have a sore throat.

2. Which of these sentences use the past perfect? Write down the sentences.
   a. We had chips for tea.
   b. Tilly had thought that playing a trick on Mrs Parker was a good idea.
   c. Fatima had a beautiful new bicycle.
   d. We had gone to the beach first.
   e. Mr Carter had forgotten the hockey sticks.
   f. The chicken had ten chicks.

3. Write these sentences, completing them with a present perfect verb. Remember, the first word you write will need to be either 'have' or 'has'.
   a. Ow. That bee _____ me!
   b. The sun _____ over the fence.
   c. The major _____ an award to the firefighters for their bravery.
   d. Jude _____ a writing competition.
   e. "Look! It _____ to snow!"
   f. The ice skater _____ and twisted her ankle.

4. Complete these past tense sentences using the past perfect. Remember: the verb will need to start with 'had'.
   a. We _____ half way to Granny's when we realised we had forgotten the baby.
   b. Stephanie _____ to learn French.
   c. Manuel _____ when the bell went.
   d. Our money _____ so we decided to go home.
   e. We _____ the dishes and were ready to go.
   f. The balloon _____ all the way to Australia.

Grammatical words 9

100 English Lessons Year 5 links:

- Starter activity 17 (page 15): The perfect form
- Autumn 1, Week 1 (page 20): Lesson 2, Creating an impact

Year 5 Practice Book links:

- (page 56): Using the perfect form of verbs
- (page 57): When and why?

Modal verbs and Adverbs of possibility

Prior learning

- Know that a verb is a doing word.
- Know that an adverb tells you more about a verb and often ends in 'ly'.

Learn

- Explain to the children that modal verbs and adverbs of possibility are often used in speech and can give subtle differences to the overall meaning. You may wish to cover modal verbs and adverbs of possibility in two separate sessions initially.
- Offer them some sentences which you then discuss with them – asking the children to identify which words tell them how likely or certain something is. For instance:
  - I **can** teach brilliantly.
  - I **could** teach brilliantly if you would always listen perfectly.
  - I **may** let you go for your break if you work hard.
  - **Maybe** we'll do some work, maybe we **won't**.
  - You are **definitely** going to do all of the work I set you.
  - This is **possibly** the most interesting lesson you will ever have the pleasure to attend.

Curriculum objectives

- To use modal verbs or adverbs to indicate degrees of possibility.

Success criteria

- I can use different modal verbs and adverbs of possibility.
- I can understand how they can change the meaning of a sentence.

- Discuss what the children would like to do in life. It could be what might happen today, at the weekend or as a lifetime ambition for when they are older. Point out the modal verbs you have used to introduce the discussion ('would', 'could', 'might') and write them on the board. Point out differences in levels of certainty; for instance, 'You must join in with the discussion' is quite different to and stronger than 'You could join in…'.

- As volunteers offer their contributions, isolate and talk about the modal verbs or adverbs of possibility used, writing them on the board. For instance, if someone says 'I might go to my friend's house after school', explore how certain they are and how that certainty could change if they were to use a different modal verb such as 'I will go'. Keep the discussion going until all nine modal verbs are up on the board.

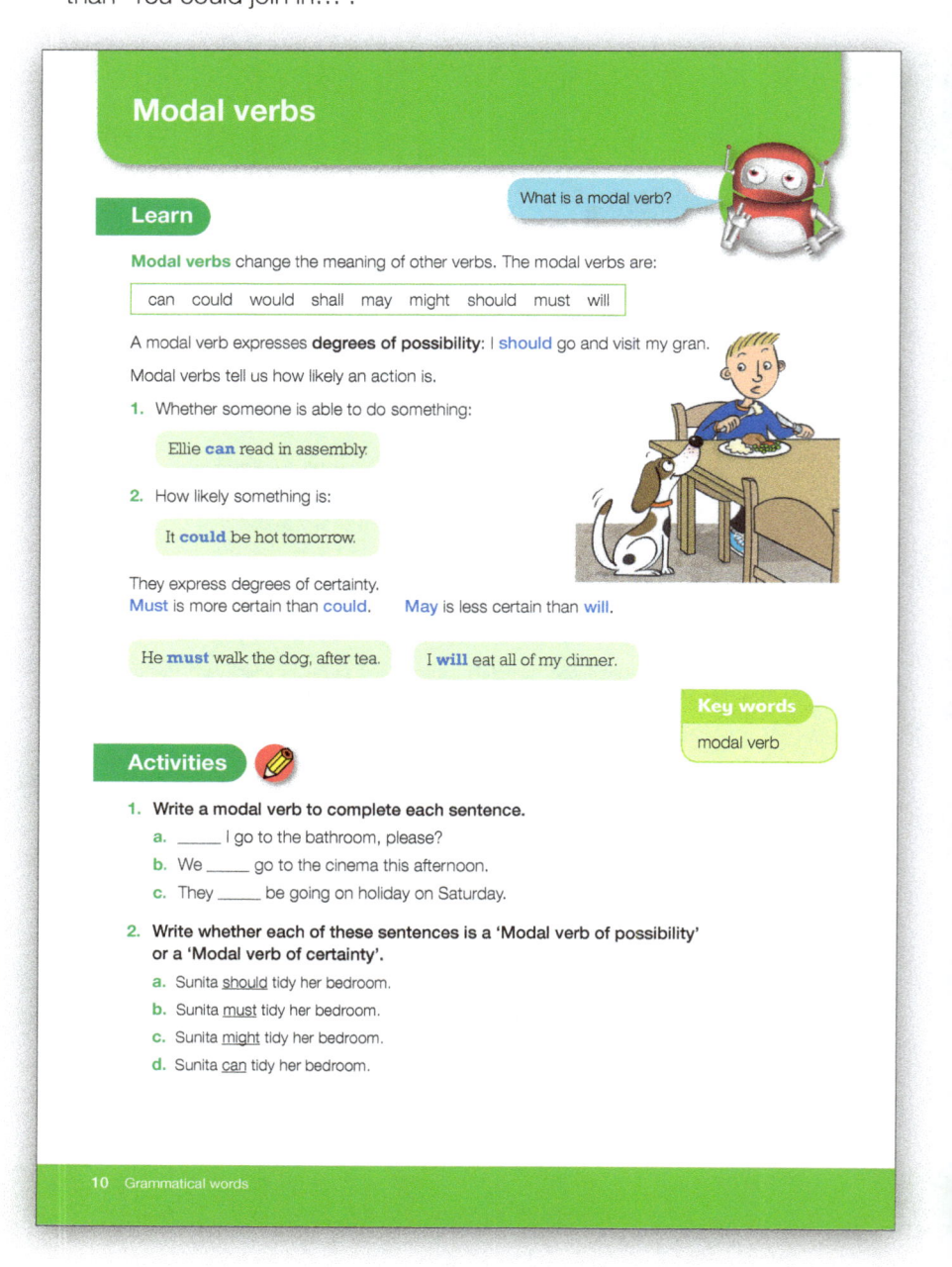

Modal verbs

Learn

What is a modal verb?

Modal verbs change the meaning of other verbs. The modal verbs are:

| can | could | would | shall | may | might | should | must | will |

A modal verb expresses **degrees of possibility**: I should go and visit my gran.
Modal verbs tell us how likely an action is.

1. Whether someone is able to do something:

   Ellie **can** read in assembly.

2. How likely something is:

   It **could** be hot tomorrow.

They express degrees of certainty.
Must is more certain than **could**.   **May** is less certain than **will**.

He **must** walk the dog, after tea.   I **will** eat all of my dinner.

Key words

modal verb

Activities

1. Write a modal verb to complete each sentence.
   a. _____ I go to the bathroom, please?
   b. We _____ go to the cinema this afternoon.
   c. They _____ be going on holiday on Saturday.

2. Write whether each of these sentences is a 'Modal verb of possibility' or a 'Modal verb of certainty'.
   a. Sunita should tidy her bedroom.
   b. Sunita must tidy her bedroom.
   c. Sunita might tidy her bedroom.
   d. Sunita can tidy her bedroom.

10 Grammatical words

Talk

- Ask the children to work in pairs, putting the modal verbs into an ordinary conversation between the two of them. Ask them also to explore how things can become more or less certain, depending on which ones they use.
- Working with a partner, ask the children to write a script, choosing what levels of possibility and certainty they are going to put across between someone who is in a position of power and someone who ought to obey that power. It could be: a teacher and a child; a parent and child; a police officer and a member of the public; a doctor and a patient; a head teacher and a member of staff; a boss and a worker. Ask them to experiment with modal verbs and adverbs of possibility – perhaps the power is strongly in one direction; perhaps the weaker character grows stronger; perhaps both characters are very certain about what they want. Ask confident pairs to perform and use this as the basis for further discussion.

Activities

- Use the activities in the textbook and on pages 58–60 of the *Year 5 Practice Book* to consolidate understanding.

Write

- Ask the children to write nine true sentences about themselves, using a different modal verb in each one.
- Ask the children to write eight true sentences about themselves, using a different adverb of possibility in each one.

Adverbs of possibility

Learn

What is an adverb of possibility?

An **adverb** describes a verb. It tells us *how* something was done.

| probably   perhaps   maybe   certainly   definitely |
| obviously   clearly   possibly |

Maybe and **perhaps** usually come at the beginning of a sentence or clause.

> **Perhaps** our visitors will arrive soon.
> **Maybe** we can go for a walk, if it stops raining.

Other adverbs of possibility usually come in front of the main verb.

> They **probably** will be going to France this summer.

However, they come after the verbs **am**, **is**, **are**, **was** and **were**.

> We are **definitely** going to the party.

Activities

1. Copy each sentence, choose an appropriate adverb of possibility to complete each.

   | maybe   probably   obviously |

   a. Opposite sides of a rectangle are ___ equal lengths.
   b. ___ the water will be warm enough to swim in.
   c. There is ___ enough petrol in the car.

2. Write a sentence, using an adverb of possibility.

Key words
adverb

Grammatical words 11

---

100 English Lessons Year 5 links:

- Starter activity 16 (page 15): Indicating degrees of possibility
- Autumn 1, Week 2 (pages 22–24): use verbs and adverbs for expressing opinions
- Summer 1, Week 3 (page 155): Lesson 4, Dynamic language
- Summer 2, Week 2 (pages 182–184): use modal verbs and adverbs for persuasive purposes

Year 5 Practice Book links:

- (pages 58–60): How likely is it?

Year 5 Grammatical words   17

Relative clauses

Prior learning

- Understand the difference between nouns and pronouns.

Learn

- Use starter activity 3, 'Relative pronouns' from *100 English Lessons Year 5* as an introduction to relative pronouns.
- Give examples of sentences which contain relative clauses and introduce and explore each of the relative pronouns 'who', 'which', 'where', 'when', 'whose' and 'that'.
- Explore the use of commas which are often used to enclose relative clauses.
- Once the children have understood the concept of relative clauses and pronouns, you may wish to introduce the idea of implied relative pronouns. The *Year 5 Practice Book* provides reinforcement for implied relative pronouns.

Talk

- Ask the children to work in pairs or threes. Tell them to make up simple sentences about their lives and their family. For instance, 'My mum works in a bank' or 'My house is near to the school'. Then to add a relative clause such as, 'My mum, who is very good with money, works in a bank' or 'My house, which has a lovely garden, is near to the school'. Tell them that for this exercise the sentences can be imaginary – the important part is to use relative pronouns and relative clauses; they may find it easier to create non-factual examples.
- Invite sets of five children to the front to act out the sentences from activity 1 in the textbook. Arrange them in a line and give them tasks:

  1. You're the first part of the sentence

  2. You're a comma – either say the word 'comma' aloud, do an action, or both

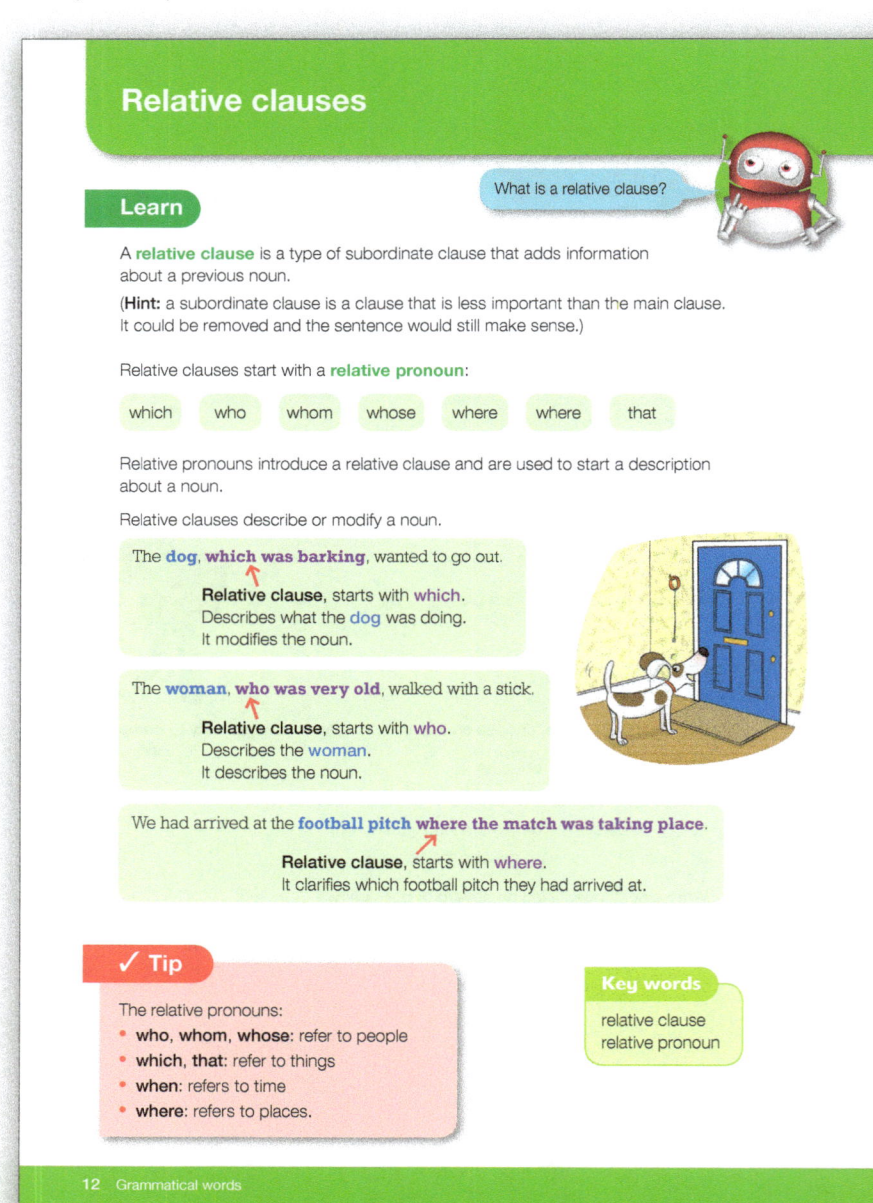

Curriculum objectives

- To use relative clauses beginning with 'who', 'which', 'where', 'when', 'whose', 'that' or with an implied (omitted) relative pronoun.

Success criteria

- I can identify and use relative pronouns.
- I can identify and create relative clauses.

Relative clauses

Learn

What is a relative clause?

A **relative clause** is a type of subordinate clause that adds information about a previous noun.

(**Hint:** a subordinate clause is a clause that is less important than the main clause. It could be removed and the sentence would still make sense.)

Relative clauses start with a **relative pronoun**:

| which | who | whom | whose | where | where | that |

Relative pronouns introduce a relative clause and are used to start a description about a noun.

Relative clauses describe or modify a noun.

The **dog**, **which was barking**, wanted to go out.

> **Relative clause**, starts with **which**.
> Describes what the **dog** was doing.
> It modifies the noun.

The **woman**, **who was very old**, walked with a stick.

> **Relative clause**, starts with **who**.
> Describes the **woman**.
> It describes the noun.

We had arrived at the **football pitch where the match was taking place**.

> **Relative clause**, starts with **where**.
> It clarifies which football pitch they had arrived at.

✓ Tip

The relative pronouns:
- **who, whom, whose**: refer to people
- **which, that**: refer to things
- **when**: refers to time
- **where**: refers to places.

Key words

relative clause
relative pronoun

12 Grammatical words

3. You're the relative clause – say the relative pronoun a bit louder than the rest of the clause
4. You're a comma
5. You're the final part of the sentence.

- Encourage the actors to make it fun to watch by adding facial expressions, tone of voice and body movements. Challenge the audience to remove part of the sentence while leaving something that still makes sense.

Activities

- Use the activities in the textbook and on pages 61–64 of the *Year 5 Practice Book* to consolidate understanding.
- To extend creative learning from activity 3, use *100 English Lessons Year 5* photocopiable page 76.

Write

- Ask the children to create their own sentences to cover different types of relative clause and relative pronoun. Tell them that it could be the opening of a story.

> Relative clauses are often enclosed by commas. They start with a relative pronoun.

Activities

1. Write the relative clause in each sentence.
   a. The weather forecast, which we were listening to, told us there would be snow.
   b. The man, whose window it was, said it would need to be repaired.
   c. The pitch, where the game was to be played, was waterlogged.
   d. My toe, which Sophie had trodden on, began to throb.

2. Write the noun that the relative clause is about.
   a. The sofa, which needed re-covering, was very comfortable.
   b. My sister Josie, when she is not on her phone, is quite friendly.
   c. That is the girl who stole my bike.
   d. Simon told a joke that was really funny.

3. Write the missing relative pronoun.
   a. Look – that's the player _____ scored the goal.
   b. The volcano, _____ everyone thought was dormant, erupted.
   c. I can't find the book _____ I know I had yesterday.

4. Write these sentences as one sentence using a relative clause.
   a. Katerina is coming to dinner. She is my new best friend.
   b. The corner shop is opening tomorrow. It has been closed for a refit.
   c. The weather is lovely in Dubai. I have been in Dubai this week.
   d. We took care on the road. The road was bumpy.

5. These sentences make sense, but write the relative pronoun that the writer has implied.
   a. This is the new girl _____ I told you about.
   b. Paul has the book _____ Cameron lent me.
   c. Let's go to the shop _____ Finn told me about.
   d. We avoided the path _____ Granny fell over on last time.

✓ Tip

In some sentences, the relative pronoun is omitted but the sentence still makes sense.
The man [who] I was talking to was very nice.
We don't need the word **who** in this sentence because it is implied.

100 English Lessons Year 5 links:

- Starter activity 3 (page 11): Relative pronouns
- Autumn 2, Week 2 (page 56): Lesson 4, Clauses
- Autumn 2, Week 3 (page 59): Lesson 4, Writing a character profile
- Autumn 2, Assess and review (page 69): Relative clauses
- Spring 1, Week 2 (page 88): Lesson 5, Pronouns, commas and relative clauses
- Spring 1, Week 5 (page 96): Lesson 2, Adding to sentences

Year 5 Practice Book links:

- (pages 61–62): All in a good clause
- (pages 63–64): It's all relative

Commas to clarify meaning

Prior learning

- Understand the basic building blocks of simple sentences.

Learn

- Look at some written examples of sentences with and without commas (for example, those provided in the textbook). Ask the children if they can identify the differences between them and their different meanings.
- Together, think of other examples with and without commas that mean different things.
- Explain to the children that, in speech, we can use intonation and pausing to make our meaning clear. Practise saying the sentences in different ways with and without commas to see the difference.
- Further ideas for introducing commas to clarify meaning are provided in *100 English Lessons Year 5 Starter activity 15* and *Autumn 2, Week 2, Lesson 5*.

Commas to clarify meaning

Learn

How are commas used to clarify meaning?

Commas are placed in sentences to help us understand the meaning of something. Using commas within a sentence can help make the meaning clearer and avoid ambiguity.

Sometimes the meaning isn't clear without commas.
In the following sentences the words are the same but the comma makes the meaning different.

"Can we go to see Gran?"

Someone is asking if we can go to see Gran.

"Can we go to see, Gran?"

Gran is being asked if we can go to see something.

The comma alters the meaning.
In the next two sentences, the commas alter the meaning.

My mother says Shona is beautiful.

My mother is saying that Shona is beautiful.

My mother, says Shona, is beautiful.

Shona is saying that her mother is beautiful.

In this sentence, which is a list, commas separate the individual items.

I like mince, pies and apples.

Without the comma the meaning is different.

I like mince pies and apples.

Key words

comma

Curriculum objectives

- To use commas to clarify meaning or avoid ambiguity in writing.

Success criteria

- I can use commas within a sentence to clarify meaning.

Talk

- Using short texts, invite pairs of children out to the front. One reads the words, the other looks out for the commas, both saying the word 'comma' and doing their own funny action to go with it. With careful preparation, the exercise could also be used to show how the sentence meaning changes if the comma is not used.

Activities

- Use the activities in the textbook and on pages 75–78 of the *Year 5 Practice Book* to consolidate understanding.
- Page 77 of the *Year 5 Practice Book*, provides a suitable exercise for reinserting commas.
- Having completed the textbook activities, ask the children to take a look at how commas can help to clarify meaning in the work they have done. Also ask them to note how, when writing, a lack of commas could lead to confusion or hilarity.

Activities

1. Write each of the sentences below and next to each one write the sentence from the box that matches the meaning.

   > It's time to go silly.
   > It's time to go, silly.
   > Please stop hitting Tamara.
   > Please stop hitting, Tamara.
   > Sam loves cooking animals and fast cars.
   > Sam loves cooking, animals and fast cars.

   a. You silly person – it's time to go.
   b. Stop hitting a child called Tamara.
   c. Sam loves cooking. He also loves animals and he loves fast cars.
   d. Sam loves cooking animals. He also loves cooking fast cars.
   e. It's time to start acting in a silly way.
   f. Tamara – please can you stop hitting people.

2. Write the meaning of these sentences.

   a. Tell your cousin Alex.
   b. Tell your cousin, Alex.
   c. Shall we eat Donna?
   d. Shall we eat, Donna?
   e. I made some decorations out of silver paper and glue.
   f. I made some decorations out of silver, paper and glue.

3. Write these sentences, adding commas – or not – to make the meaning clear.

   a. It's your turn to hide Bunny. (Meaning: It's Bunny's turn to hide.)
   b. Julie says my mother should know better. (Meaning: My mother says that Julie should know better.)
   c. The dog barked suddenly hearing the doorbell ring. (Meaning: The dog barked because he had suddenly heard the doorbell ring.)
   d. We bought some peanut butter biscuits chocolate milk and some apples. (Meaning: We bought some peanut butter and some biscuits and some chocolate milk and some apples.)
   e. The teacher says Sophie is cross. (Meaning: The teacher says that Sophie is cross.)

Punctuation 15

---

100 English Lessons Year 5 links:

- Starter activity 15 (page 15): Commas for clarity
- Autumn 2, Week 2 (page 56): Lesson 5, Commas for clarity
- Autumn 2, Week 3 (page 59): Lesson 4, Writing a character profile
- Spring 1, Week 2 (page 88): Lesson 5, Pronouns, commas and relative clauses
- Spring 1, Week 3 (page 90): Lesson 3, Adding to a sentence

Year 5 Practice Book links:

- (pages 75–76): Crystal clear commas
- (page 77): Adding commas
- (page 78): Punctuating Rapunzel

Year 5 Punctuation

Parenthesis

Prior learning

- Understand usage of relative pronouns and relative clauses.

Learn

- Use starter activity 5 from *100 English Lessons Year 5* to help introduce this topic.
- Ensure that children understand that parenthesis is the information inserted into the sentence which is used with punctuation and not the punctuation itself. You may wish to focus initially on the use of brackets and then introduce the use of commas and dashes later, this is the approach of *100 English Lessons Year 5*.
- Give some examples of sentences with parenthesis that are missing the punctuation and ask the children to come up and insert it. Discuss how this helps the sentence make sense and also, how the parenthesis information is extra.
- Explore how the parenthesis information is additional – try removing parenthesis from a sentence, it should still make sense.

Curriculum objectives

- To use brackets, dashes or commas to indicate parenthesis.

Success criteria

- I can use parenthesis, employing brackets, commas or dashes.

Parenthesis

Learn

What is parenthesis?

Parenthesis is the term used for a word, clause or phrase that is inserted into a sentence to provide more detail.
- Parenthesis is what is written inside **brackets**.
- **Commas** and **dashes** can do the same job as brackets.

The following sentence gives a small piece of information:

> My sister is getting married next week.

By adding parenthesis, more detail is given but the meaning remains the same:

> My sister (who is older than me) is getting married next week.

parenthesis with brackets

Commas and pairs of dashes can do the same job as brackets.

> My sister, who is older than me, is getting married next week.

parenthesis with commas

> My sister – who is older than me – is getting married next week.

parenthesis with dashes

Dashes tend to be used in less formal writing, such as in an email.

Remember, parenthesis is the information you add, not the punctuation around it.

Key words

parenthesis
brackets
dash
comma

- Point out that the example in the textbook uses 'who is older than me' as parenthesis. Challenge the class to recall what kind of pronoun and clause is being used. Once the relative pronouns have been recalled, ask if anyone can think of a different parenthesis using either the same relative pronoun or a different one. For example, 'My sister, who is very beautiful, is getting married next week'.

Activities

- Use the activities in the textbook and on pages 79–81 of the *Year 5 Practice Book* to consolidate understanding.
- Give out a list of short sentences and ask the children to make up parentheses for them. Tell them that relative pronouns and relative clauses may prove very useful to them, but that other words and phrases will also work.
- *100 English Lessons Year 5* photocopiable page 138 'Dashes' provides a support activity.

Write

- Ask the children to write a descriptive passage about a spooky house which might be the opening of a story. Challenge them to include different examples of parenthesis in their sentences. The beginning might be: 'Gruesome Grange, an old house by the river, was the scariest place in town.'

Activities

1. a. Rewrite the sentence and insert the parenthesis into the following sentence, using brackets.
   Toby was lost for seven days. **Parenthesis**: *a six-year-old collie dog*
   b. Rewrite the sentence and insert the parenthesis into the correct place in the following sentence, using commas.
   There are many ways to climb Mount Snowdon. **Parenthesis**: *most of them difficult*
   c. Rewrite the sentence and insert the parenthesis into the correct place in the following sentence, using dashes.
   'Grab a piece of my heart' will be number one next week. **Parenthesis**: *such a great song*
   d. Rewrite the sentence and insert Parenthesis 1 and Parenthesis 2 into the correct places in the following sentence using dashes and commas.
   My new book is going to be a best seller.
   Parenthesis 1: *Wheelchair Warrior*
   Parenthesis 2: *according to my publisher*
2. Rewrite this sentence without the parenthesis.
   Our favourite place – it's so romantic – is Venice.

100 English Lessons Year 5 links:

- Starter activity 5 (page 12): Parenthesis
- Spring 1, Week 3 (page 91): Lesson 4, Brackets
- Spring 1, Assess and review (page 101): Brackets
- Spring 2, Week 3 (page 123): Lesson 5, Parenthesis

Year 5 Practice Book links:

- (page 79–80): Perfect parentheses
- (page 81): Phantom phrases

Using hyphens

Prior learning

- Understand the word 'prefix' and its function.
- Know what a root word is.

Learn

- Explain to the children that when a prefix ends with the same vowel as at the beginning of the root word, writers often prefer to use a hyphen for clarity, even though the unhyphenated version would also be correct. *Co-ordinate* versus *coordinate* is a good example of this. When the joining vowels are different, a writer may be likely to choose the unhyphenated version of the spelling. For example, *proactive* being preferred to *pro-active*.

- Tell them that they have quite a lot of freedom when connecting prefixes to root words. *Antiaircraft*, for instance is perfectly correct, but most writers would make a personal decision that it looks funny and would insert the hyphen for *anti-aircraft*.

- Talk to them also about house style, telling them how organisations such as newspapers will decide upon their own 'correct' versions of all sorts of things, including hyphenation. If they were to one day get a job with such an organisation, they would have to make sure they used the 'correct' version of hyphenated words.

- Explain how hyphens can also help to clarify meaning, for example joining two words that act as one word. Review the examples in the textbook.

- Hyphenation can also change over time and through common

Curriculum objectives

- To use hyphens to avoid ambiguity.

Success criteria

- I can use hyphens in different ways to make the meaning clear.

Using hyphens

Learn

What is a hyphen?

Hyphens with prefix

When we join a **prefix** that ends with a vowel to a **root word** that begins with a vowel, it can create a word that looks peculiar. To make the word clearer we can use a **hyphen** between the prefix and the root.

co + opt = co-opt (instead of coopt)
re + enter = re-enter (rather than reenter)

Sometimes we use a hyphen if the prefix plus the root word has two meanings:

re-cover – to cover again
recover – to get over something

Key words

prefix
root word
hyphen

Using hyphens for clarity

We use a hyphen to join numbers and to join words that act like one word.

We use a hyphen to join two adjectives that are working together to create one idea:

man-eating shark   blue-green coat   fifty-five freckles

We use a hyphen to join two words to make some compound words.

Sam has a great grandmother who is fantastic and a great-grandmother who is ancient.

Would you like me to blow-dry your hair?

It should be remembered that sometimes words can be correctly spelled with both a hyphen and without one.

For example, the spelling **co-ordinate** and **coordinate** are both considered to be correct. Using the hyphen for this word is a matter of style and choice.

*Hyphens can disappear over time through usage, for example the word **today** used to be spelled **to-day**.*

18 Punctuation

usage. Tell them that the words *today* and *tomorrow* were once spelled *to-day* and *to-morrow* and that *bumble-bee* is now commonly accepted as being spelled *bumblebee*.

- Use the activities in *100 English Lessons Year 5* to reinforce learning.

Activities

- Use the activities in the textbook and on pages 20–21 and 83 of the *Year 5 Practice Book* to consolidate understanding of the two uses of hyphens.
- As ongoing research into the fascinating subject of hyphenation, the children could be tasked with finding examples of hyphenation in books, newspapers and leaflets. Perhaps an organic collage called 'The Great Hyphen Hunt' could be created, where examples are built up over a few weeks.
- Have fun creating compound adjectives. Give the children some commonly used ones such as *red-hot* and *ice-cold* and challenge them to create some new ones. Ask them to put them into sentences and say them to each other. Which ones work best? Which ones could catch on?

Activities

1. **Combine the suffix and root word with a hyphen. Write the word.**
   a. re + enact
   b. co + own
   c. co + opt
   d. re + educate
   e. re + emphasise
   f. re + energise
   g. re + examining

2. **Choose the correct or preferred spelling. Write the word.**
   a. The third form **re-elected/reelected** Pushkal as form captain.
   b. Daisy went to the office to **re-claim/reclaim** her jumper.
   c. The fox waited for the rabbit to **re-emerge/reemerge** from its hole.
   d. Mrs Thompson told the children to go back out and **re-enter/reenter** the classroom without pushing and shoving.
   e. The magician made the rabbit **dis-appear/disappear**.
   f. The chair needed to be **re-covered/recovered** after the twins' party.
   g. It took me a long time to **re-cover/recover** from the flu.

3. **Rewrite these sentences, adding a hyphen to join words where necessary.**
   a. The swimmers plunged into the ice cold water.
   b. We ran out into the snow covered garden.
   c. Kuba slowly saved up twenty five pounds.
   d. Watch out – the iron is red hot.
   e. We decided that the chocolate coated raisins were one of our five a day.
   f. The cottage looked very run down.
   g. My sister's bedroom is a definite no go area.

Punctuation 19

100 English Lessons Year 5 links:

- Starter activity 1 (page 11): Hyphens
- Autumn 1, Week 5 (page 33): Lesson 4, Hyphens
- Autumn 1, Assess and review (page 37): Hyphens

Year 5 Practice Book links:

- (pages 20–21): Prefixes with hyphens
- (page 83): Helpful hyphens

Year 5 Punctuation 25

Using a colon

Prior learning

- Know how to separate the items in a list with commas.

Learn

- Introduce colons to introduce a list and to introduce explanations. This may take several sessions and you may wish to deal each usage separately. (You may also wish to link this to bullet points, see page 27 of this book.)
- Once the children understand the usages, provide sales leaflets where colons are used in the two different ways – for lists and for explanation. Go through the examples carefully, examining which purpose each usage is for.
- Play 'Colleen' as a whole class. Make a huge colon on card. Decorate it to look like 'Colleen'.
- Prepare openings for sentences, some for lists, some for explanations. Tell the class whether it's going to be a list or an explanation. Invite two children to the front, child one reads the prepared opener and child two either shouts out 'colon' in a silly voice or holds up 'Colleen' while the class shout out 'colon'. If it's a list, ask the class to offer items on that list or if it's an explanation, ask the class for a possible second part to the sentence. For lists, a comma character could also be created or you could punctuate vocally.

Activities

- Use the activities in the textbook and on page 82 of the *Year 5 Practice Book* to consolidate understanding.

Curriculum objectives

- To use a colon to introduce a list.

Success criteria

- I can use a colon to introduce a list.
- I can use a colon to introduce an explanation.

100 English Lessons Year 5 links:

- Summer 1, Week 1 (page 148): Lesson 3, Bullet points
- Summer 1, Week 5 (page 160): Lesson 2, Comparing myths
- Summer 1, Assess and review (page 165): Bullet points
- Summer 2, Week 5 (page 191): Lesson 1, The fish that disappeared

Year 5 Practice Book links:

- (page 82): Twisted lists

Using a colon

Learn

What is a colon?

A **colon** is a punctuation mark that introduces a list or an explanation.
It looks like this :

Colons for lists
You can learn many instruments at our school: guitar, ukulele, djembe, saxophone, keyboard and many more.
We had every type of weather on holiday: snow, sun, wind and rain.

Colons for explanation
I'm sorry we're so late: our bus broke down.
The pudding was superb: chocolate cake and cream!

Key words
colon

Activities

1. Are these colons introducing an explanation or a list? Write each sentence and then 'explanation' or 'list' after it.
   a. Football club was cancelled: Mr Stevens was off sick.
   b. Go and get everything you need: your PE bag, your lunch box, your homework and your house keys.
   c. Akua was looking forward to her party: they were going tubing at the ski slope.
   d. Rahul said he wanted three friends to come over: Arjun, Tim and Raj.

2. Write these sentences adding a colon to each one to make it clearer.
   a. Don't sit on the wall the top bricks are loose.
   b. Practise both your piano pieces 'Rowing boat' and 'Lullaby'.

3. Write out and complete these sentences using your own ideas.
   a. Mum didn't mind when John broke the vase:
   b. I have three things to do before school:
   c. Wednesday is my favourite day of the week:

Bullet points

Prior learning

- Identify the use of bullet points in non-fiction texts.

Learn

- You may wish to link 'Using a colon' on page 26 of this book with introducing bullet points.
- Explore the use of bullet points and how they can be used to express information concisely. Focus on how they should be punctuated, see the textbook. Look at examples.

Activities

- Use the activities in the textbook and on pages 84–85 of the *Year 5 Practice Book* to consolidate understanding.
- Ask the children to think about one room in their house and write a list, using bullet points of what the room contains. Remind them to be consistent, particularly with the choice of lower case or capital letters.

Write

- Challenge the children to write a leaflet explaining how to use bullet points. The explanation should take the form of a bullet-pointed list.

Bullet points

Learn

When do we use bullet points?

Bullet points are a very clear way to write a list.
They are excellent for use in non-fiction writing.

When we write a bulleted list we:
- introduce the list with a colon
- use all capitals or all small letters for the first letter of each point
- don't use 'and' at the end of a point
- use a full stop at the end of each point if it is a full sentences.

Key words
bullet point

Activities

1. Write these sentences as bulleted lists.
   a. There are three types of volcanoes: active volcanoes, dormant volcanoes and extinct volcanoes.

   b. Key facts about Michael Morpurgo: he has written over 100 books, he was Children's Laureate from 2003–2005, he runs a charity called 'Farms for City Children' and he is the author of *War Horse*.

2. Write a bulleted list of all the things you have in your school bag.

Punctuation 21

Curriculum objectives

- To punctuate bullet points consistently.

Success criteria

- I can use a colon to introduce bullet points.
- I can choose either upper or lower case for the first letter of each item.
- I can punctuate the list correctly.

100 English Lessons Year 5 links:

- Starter activity 9 (page 13): Bullet points
- Autumn 2, Week 2 (page 55): Lesson 3, How a steam engine works
- Summer 1, Week 1 (page 148): Lesson 3, Bullet points
- Summer 1, Assess and review (page 165): Bullet points
- Summer 2, Week 1 (page 181): Lesson 4, Writing reports

Year 5 Practice Book links:

- (pages 84–85): Bullet points

Year 5 Punctuation

Prefixes: 'dis' or 'mis'? and Prefixes: 're', 'de', 'over'

Prior learning

- Understand that a prefix is added to the beginning of a root word.

Learn

- Remind the children what a prefix is and recall what prefixes they already know.
- Prepare a range of verbs and prefixes. Ask the children to discuss which prefixes might work to create new words. Which ones are they sure about? Do they know what the meaning is? Encourage them to use a dictionary to check whether they are correct or not. Ask them to feed back their findings to the class.
- Remind the children of how hyphens may be used in some examples of words with prefixes, particularly when the meaning is unclear or the word looks too strange on the page (such as 're-read').
- Prepare a selection of words with prefixes which you deem will be unfamiliar to most of the children. Apply the knowledge gained to have a discussion – first in groups, then as a class – as to what the new words might mean. Tell the children that it's like detective work – they must apply prior knowledge of the root words, add in the new knowledge of the prefix and make an informed judgement as to meaning.
- The links to *100 English Lessons Year 5* provide further support.

Curriculum objectives

- To use further prefixes and suffixes and understand the guidance for adding them.
- To use verb prefixes (for example, 'dis', 'de', 'mis', 'over' and 're'). (Grammar appendix)
- To apply their growing knowledge of root words, prefixes and suffixes (morphology and etymology), as listed in the Spelling appendix, both to read aloud and to understand the meaning of new words that they meet.

Success criteria

- I can add the correct prefixes to verbs to change their meanings.

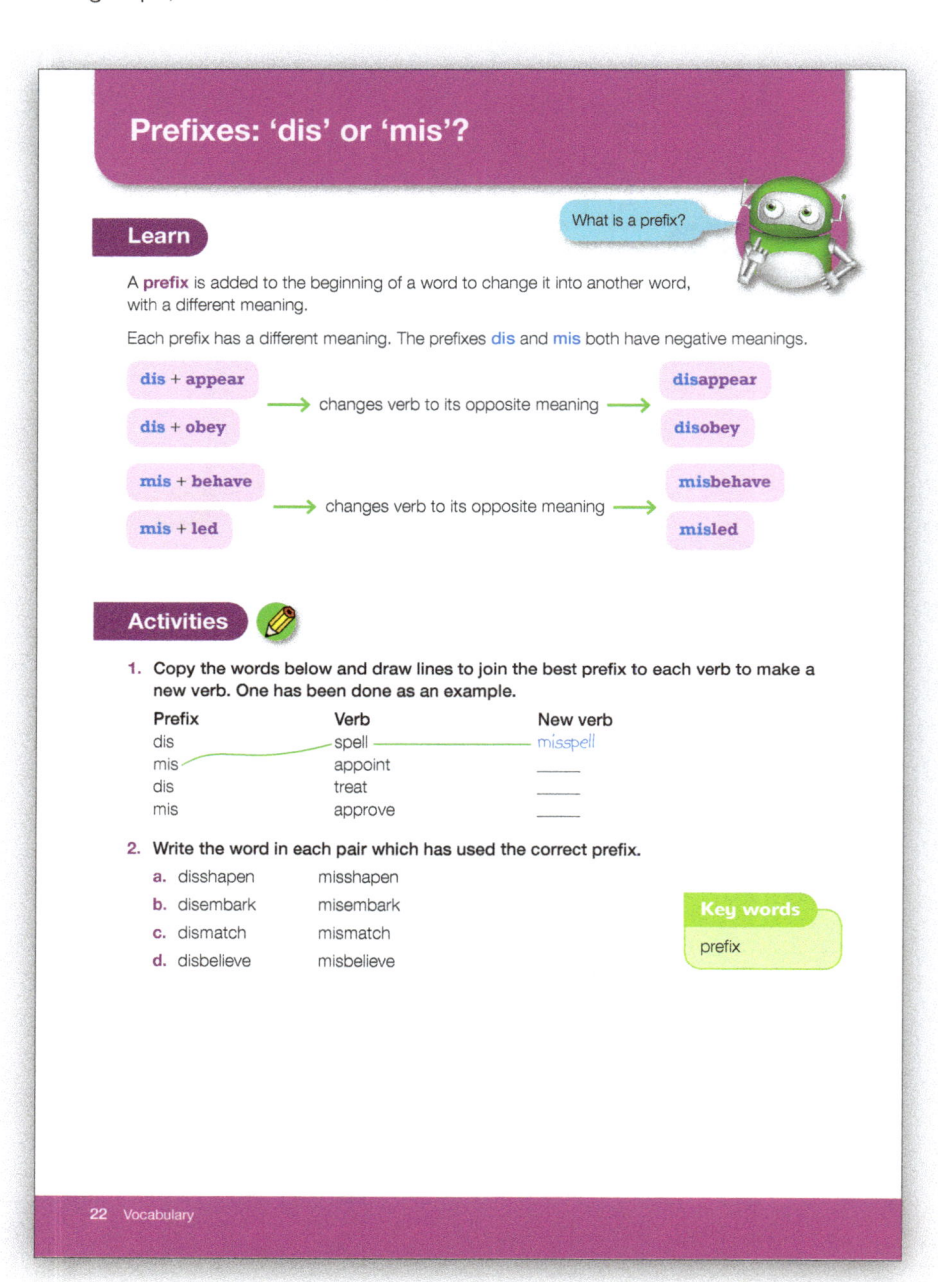

Prefixes: 'dis' or 'mis'?

Learn

What is a prefix?

A **prefix** is added to the beginning of a word to change it into another word, with a different meaning.

Each prefix has a different meaning. The prefixes *dis* and *mis* both have negative meanings.

dis + appear → changes verb to its opposite meaning → disappear
dis + obey → disobey
mis + behave → changes verb to its opposite meaning → misbehave
mis + led → misled

Activities

1. Copy the words below and draw lines to join the best prefix to each verb to make a new verb. One has been done as an example.

Prefix	Verb	New verb
dis	spell	misspell
mis	appoint	____
dis	treat	____
mis	approve	____

2. Write the word in each pair which has used the correct prefix.
   a. disshapen   misshapen
   b. disembark   misembark
   c. dismatch   mismatch
   d. disbelieve misbelieve

Key words
prefix

Activities

- Use the activities in the textbook and on page 67 of the *Year 5 Practice Book* to consolidate understanding of adding prefixes to verbs.
- The activities on pages 20–21 of the *Year 5 Practice Book* reinforce using a hyphen with prefixes and page 68 introduces more verb prefixes.
- Arranging the children in groups, ask them to use dictionaries to find verbs that begin with prefixes. Ask them to create a spidergram of the words on a large sheet. Tell them to consider carefully whether what they have found is a true prefix + verb.
- Ask each group member to be responsible for explaining one of the words found by the group. What is the prefix? What is the original verb? What did it mean before the prefix was attached? What does it mean with its prefix attached?

Write

- Write a silly opening to a story that contains as many verbs with prefixes as possible.

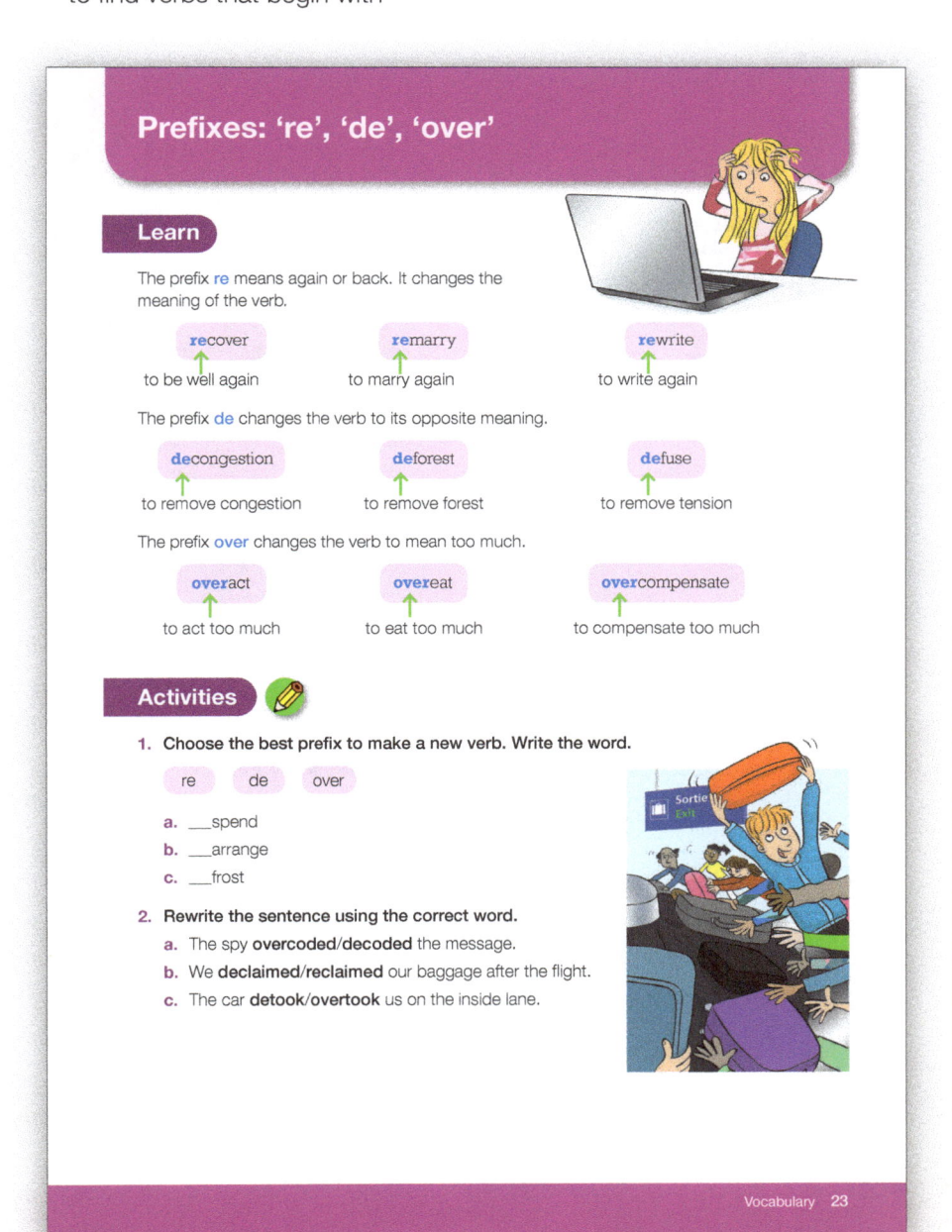

Prefixes: 're', 'de', 'over'

Learn

The prefix **re** means again or back. It changes the meaning of the verb.

- **re**cover — to be well again
- **re**marry — to marry again
- **re**write — to write again

The prefix **de** changes the verb to its opposite meaning.

- **de**congestion — to remove congestion
- **de**forest — to remove forest
- **de**fuse — to remove tension

The prefix **over** changes the verb to mean too much.

- **over**act — to act too much
- **over**eat — to eat too much
- **over**compensate — to compensate too much

Activities

1. Choose the best prefix to make a new verb. Write the word.

   re   de   over

   a. ___spend
   b. ___arrange
   c. ___frost

2. Rewrite the sentence using the correct word.
   a. The spy **overcoded**/**decoded** the message.
   b. We **declaimed**/**reclaimed** our baggage after the flight.
   c. The car **detook**/**overtook** us on the inside lane.

Vocabulary 23

---

100 English Lessons Year 5 links:

- Starter activity 8 (page 13): Make the opposite verb
- Spring 2, Week 1 (page 117): Lesson 5, Verb prefixes
- Spring 2, Assess and review (page 133): Verb prefixes

Year 5 Practice Book links:

- (pages 20–21): Prefixes with hyphens
- (page 67): Verbs and their opposites
- (page 68): More verb prefixes

Suffixes: 'ate' and Suffixes: 'ify', 'ise'

Prior learning

- Understand the difference between a noun and a verb.
- Know what an adjective is.

Learn

- Remind the children about suffixes. Introduce 'ate', 'ify' and 'ise'. You may wish to do this over several sessions or use *100 English Lessons Year 5, Autumn 2, Week 4, Lesson 1*. Ensure the children understand that some words need to be modified before adding the suffix.
- Provide a selection of fiction and factual books to groups of children. Ask them to look for words that end with 'ate', 'ise' and 'ify'. Write down the words found. Ask them to work together to discuss whether their findings truly contain suffixes – if they do, they should be able to work out which original word has been modified. They may also find that they have discovered words like *gate* and *wise* which don't fit the pattern and can be discarded for the purposes of their research.
- Have some fun making up nonsense words. Ask the children to work in pairs or threes to use simple nouns or adjectives to transform into newly-coined verbs, for which they then write

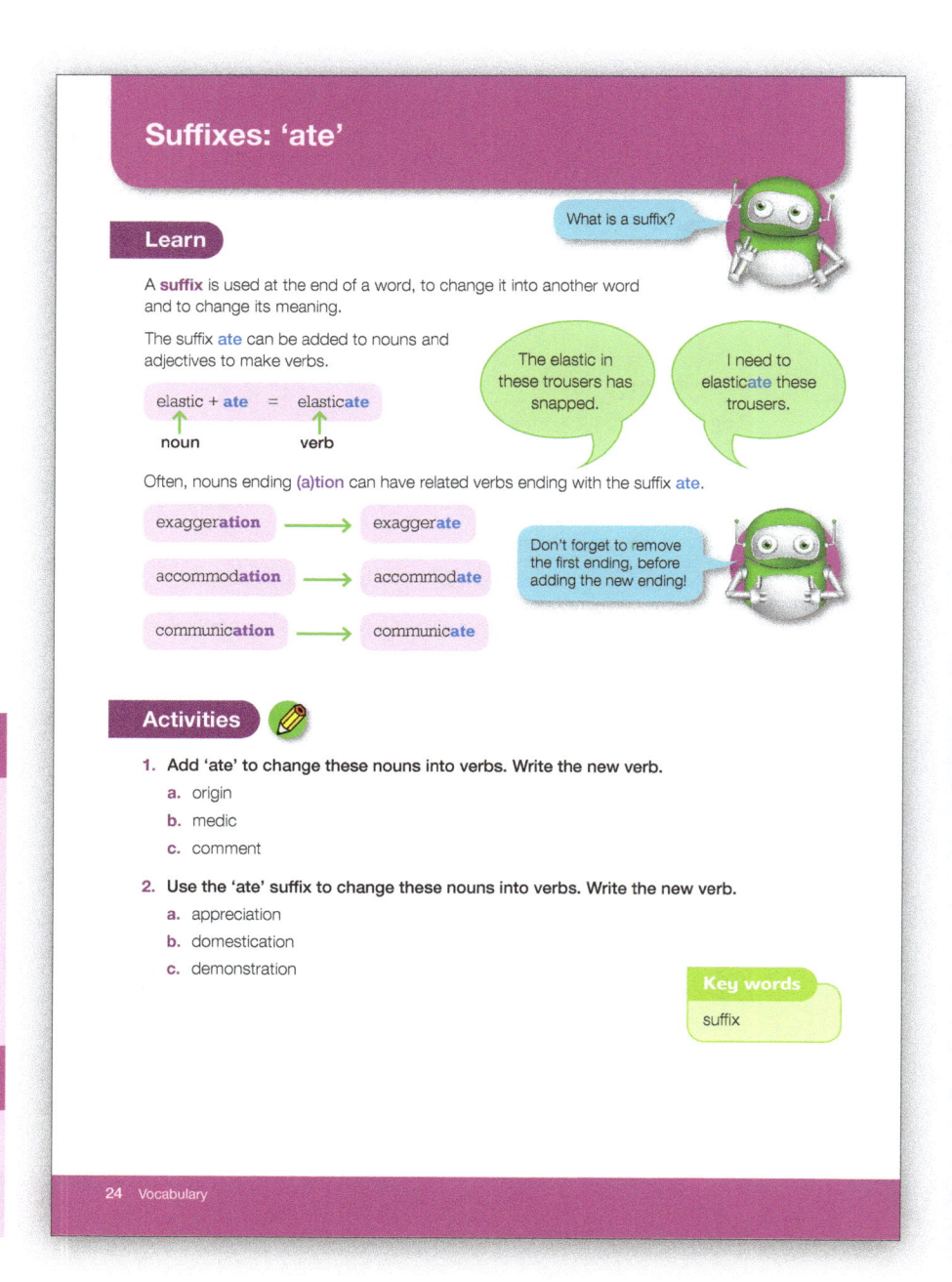

Curriculum objectives

- To use further prefixes and suffixes and understand the guidance for adding them.
- To convert nouns or adjectives into verbs using suffixes (for example, 'ate', 'ise', 'ify'). (Grammar appendix)

Success criteria

- I can convert nouns and adjectives into verbs by adding different suffixes.

Suffixes: 'ate'

What is a suffix?

Learn

A **suffix** is used at the end of a word, to change it into another word and to change its meaning.

The suffix **ate** can be added to nouns and adjectives to make verbs.

elastic + **ate** = elastic**ate**
noun → verb

The elastic in these trousers has snapped.

*I need to elastic**ate** these trousers.*

Often, nouns ending (a)**tion** can have related verbs ending with the suffix **ate**.

exagger**ation** → exagger**ate**

accommod**ation** → accommod**ate**

communic**ation** → communic**ate**

Don't forget to remove the first ending, before adding the new ending!

Activities

1. Add 'ate' to change these nouns into verbs. Write the new verb.
   a. origin
   b. medic
   c. comment

2. Use the 'ate' suffix to change these nouns into verbs. Write the new verb.
   a. appreciation
   b. domestication
   c. demonstration

Key words
suffix

24 Vocabulary

their own definition. For instance, 'hair' + 'ify' to create 'hairify', meaning to transform hair into messy hair. Ask them also to double-check in a dictionary – they may in fact be making up a word that already does exist, but which is rarely used.

Activities

- Use the activities in the textbook and on pages 65–66 of the *Year 5 Practice Book* to consolidate understanding.
- Ask the children to practise writing sentences using the verbs from the activities with the suffixes 'ate', 'ise' and 'ify'.

Suffixes: 'ify', 'ise'

Learn

The suffixes **ify** and **ise** can be added to nouns and adjectives to change them into verbs.

To attach the suffix **ify**:

pure + **ify** = pur**ify**
lose final **e**

glory + **ify** - glor**ify**
lose **y**

To attach the suffix **ise**:

apology + **ise** = apolog**ise**
lose **y**

standard + **ise** = standard**ise**
just add suffix

Activities

1. Write the correct form of the word for each sentence.
    a. The butter had started to **solidise/solidify**.
    b. The children were able to **dramatise/dramify** the story of Gelert.
    c. The farmer needed to **fertilise/fertify** his crops.

2. Change these nouns into verbs by adding a suffix. Write the new verb.
    a. individual
    b. quantity
    c. acid
    d. terror

   Don't forget to drop the y before adding an ending!

3. Change these adjectives into verbs by adding a suffix. Write the new verb.
    a. terrible
    b. popular
    c. capital

   *The **ise** suffix is a lot more common than the **ify** suffix!*

Vocabulary 25

100 English Lessons Year 5 links:

- Autumn 2, Week 4 (page 60): Lesson 1, Nouns and adjectives to verbs

Year 5 Practice Book links:

- (pages 65–66): 'Verbing' nouns and adjectives

Year 5 Vocabulary 31

Suffixes: 'able' and 'ably' and Suffixes: 'ible' and 'ibly'

Prior learning

- Know that when suffixes are added, sometimes an 'e' will get dropped.

Learn

- Recall suffixes that the children know already and the rules for adding them. Introduce 'able', 'ably', 'ible' and 'ibly' to them (you may wish to do this over more than one session).
- Look at a selection of words with these prefixes and read them aloud and sort them into groups. Can the children spot the rule? For 'able'/'ably', you can usually hear the root word still (see the textbook examples).
- Using the rules from *Year 5 Practice Book* pages 14–15 to make some wall charts where you have the rule accompanied by some examples.
- Play Able-Ible-Bingo. Provide a grid with 'able', 'ible', 'ably' and 'ibly' words listed. Read a passage of writing which contains the words. When the children hear the word read aloud, they mark it on their chart just as you would with numbers.

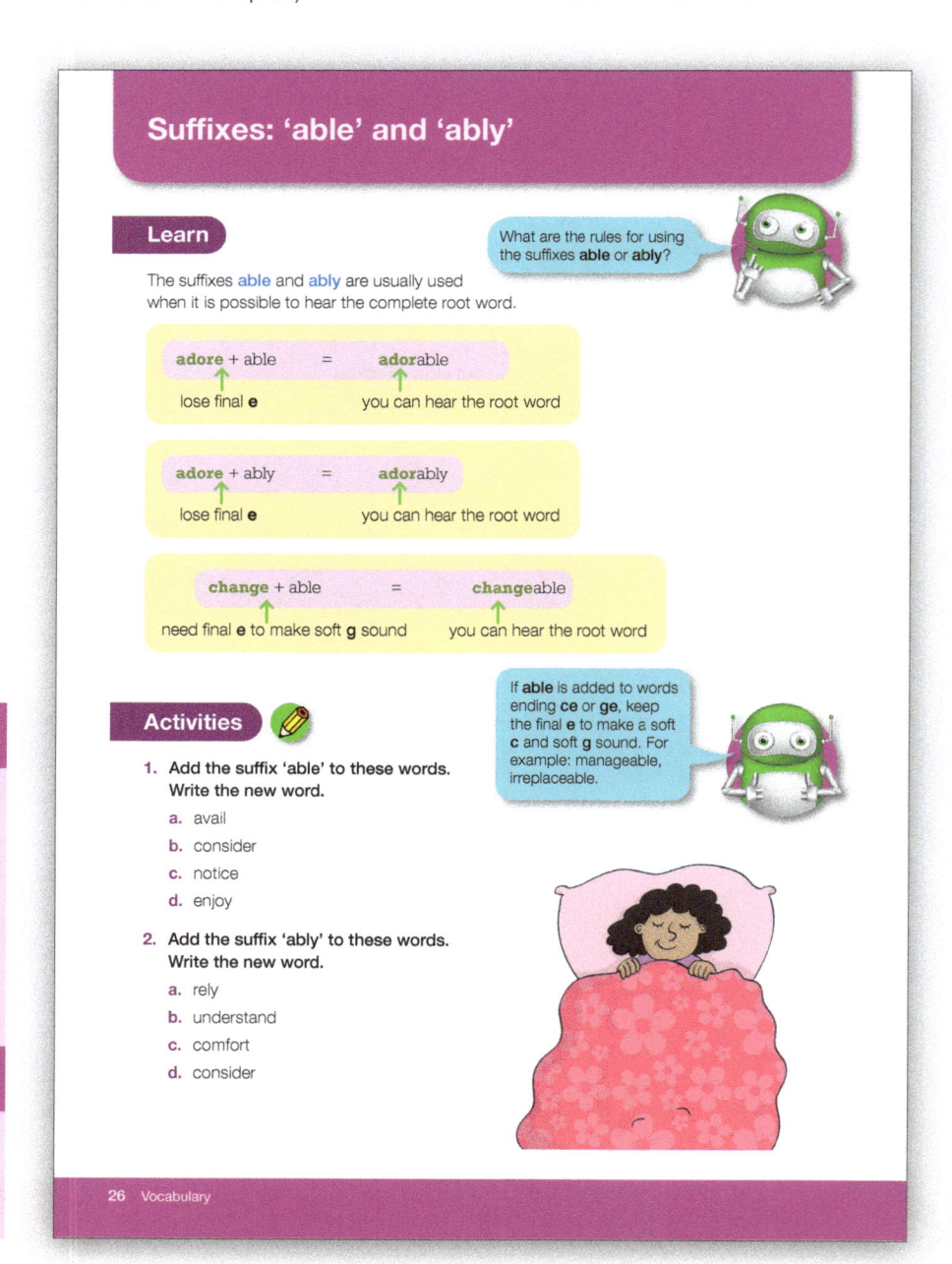

Curriculum objectives

- To use further prefixes and suffixes and understand the guidance for adding them.
- To spell words ending in 'able' and 'ible'. (Spelling appendix)
- To spell words ending in 'ably' and 'ibly'. (Spelling appendix)

Success criteria

- I can correctly spell words ending in 'able', 'ible', 'ably' and 'ibly'.

Suffixes: 'able' and 'ably'

Learn

What are the rules for using the suffixes **able** or **ably**?

The suffixes **able** and **ably** are usually used when it is possible to hear the complete root word.

adore + able = **ador**able
↑ ↑
lose final **e**   you can hear the root word

adore + ably = **ador**ably
↑ ↑
lose final **e**   you can hear the root word

change + able = **change**able
↑ ↑
need final **e** to make soft **g** sound   you can hear the root word

If **able** is added to words ending **ce** or **ge**, keep the final **e** to make a soft **c** and soft **g** sound. For example: manageable, irreplaceable.

Activities

1. Add the suffix 'able' to these words. Write the new word.
   a. avail
   b. consider
   c. notice
   d. enjoy

2. Add the suffix 'ably' to these words. Write the new word.
   a. rely
   b. understand
   c. comfort
   d. consider

Activities

- Use the activities in the textbook and on pages 14–17 of the *Year 5 Practice Book* to consolidate understanding.
- Ask the children to try to think of and list other words which end in 'able', 'ible', 'ably' and 'ibly'.
- Once the children have tackled the exercises in the *Practice Book*, ask them to use the correct spellings to write brand new sentences. Tell them to underline each usage of an 'able', 'ible', 'ably' or 'ibly' word. Tell them that, on this piece of writing, the spelling of other words is of secondary importance – if they can get the target words correct then they have succeeded.

Write

- Have fun writing part of a story, description or poem where the children are encouraged to include as many 'able', 'ible', 'ably', 'ibly' words as possible. The next challenge will be to read it aloud as it will sound like a tongue twister!

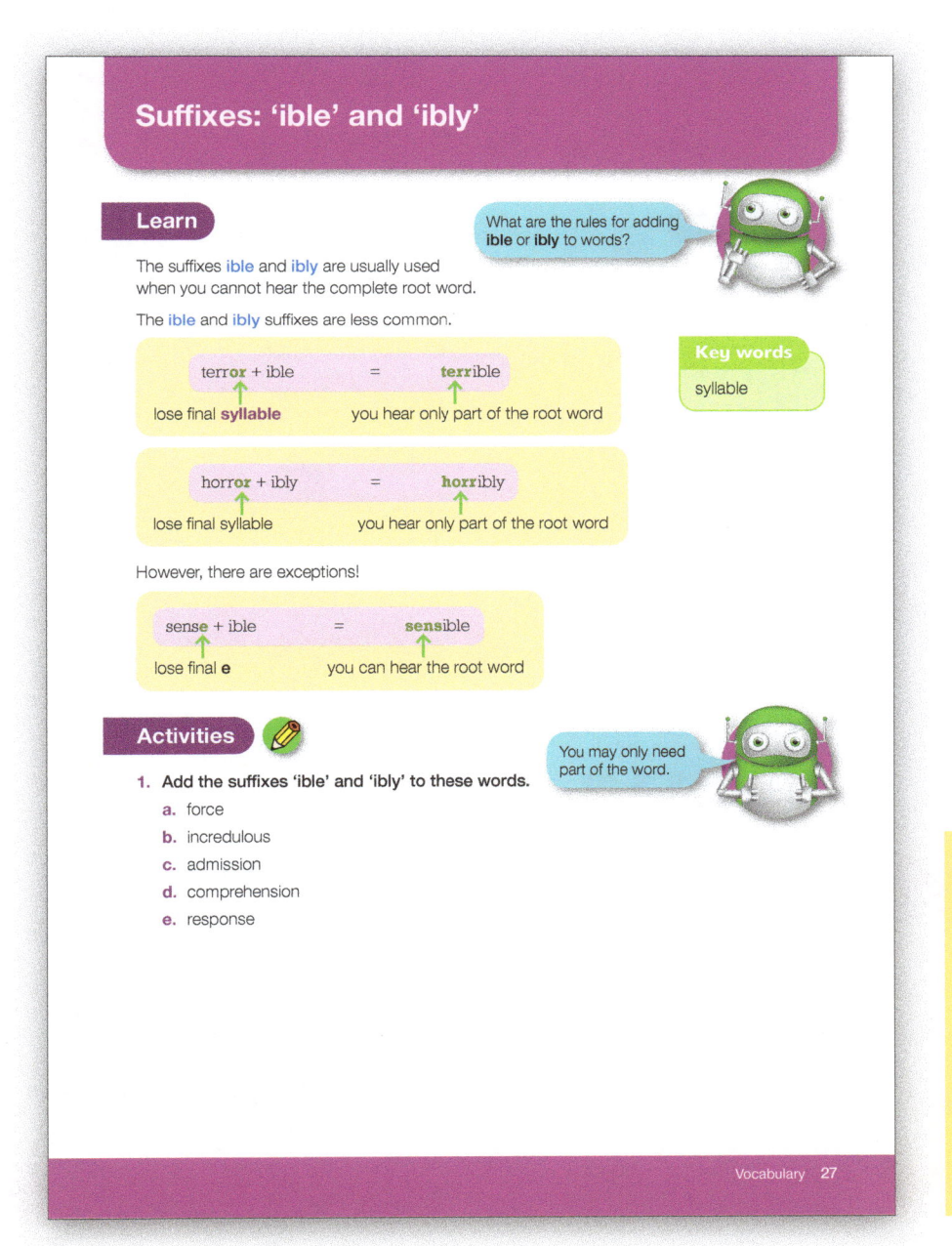

Suffixes: 'ible' and 'ibly'

Learn

What are the rules for adding **ible** or **ibly** to words?

The suffixes **ible** and **ibly** are usually used when you cannot hear the complete root word.

The **ible** and **ibly** suffixes are less common.

terr**or** + ible = te**rr**ible
lose final **syllable**   you hear only part of the root word

ho**rr**or + ibly = ho**rr**ibly
lose final syllable   you hear only part of the root word

However, there are exceptions!

sense + ible = **sens**ible
lose final **e**   you can hear the root word

Key words
syllable

Activities

You may only need part of the word.

1. Add the suffixes 'ible' and 'ibly' to these words.
   a. force
   b. incredulous
   c. admission
   d. comprehension
   e. response

Vocabulary 27

---

100 English Lessons Year 5 links:

- Autumn 1, Week 3 (page 26): Lesson 3, Adjectives ending with '-able' and '-ible'

Year 5 Practice Book links:

- (pages 14–15): Are you able?
- (pages 16–17): Fillable gaps

Adding suffixes to words ending 'fer'

Prior learning

- Know that some consonants get doubled up when adding certain suffixes.

Learn

- Write your own silly introduction to the lesson containing lots of 'fer' words and read it aloud to introduce the lesson with very exaggerated intonation on the stressed syllables and an extremely light touch on the unstressed ones. For example, 'Today children, I will be referring to some skills which will be transferred to you all. My preference for this transference…'
- Take a close look at the *Year 5 Practice Book* exercise as a whole class, using the sound of stressed syllables to help the children to hear how the spelling rules are working before they attempt to have a go on their own in writing.

Talk

- Try some very exaggerated whole-class voicing of the stressed syllables in the 'fer' verbs and their converted forms with a suffix. Make it into a chant or a silly rolling of the /rr/ sound when doubled.

Activities

- Use the activities in the textbook and on pages 18–19 of the *Year 5 Practice Book* to consolidate understanding. The *Practice Book* provide a very useful set of rules, plus a thorough practice exercise to support the learning of how to add suffixes to words ending 'fer'.
- After the *Year 5 Practice Book* exercise has been completed, ask children to work in pairs to write a script where two characters use as many 'fer' words as possible. Confident learners might give the class some real entertainment by acting out the script in an over-the-top way, putting very loud emphasis onto the doubled /rr/ sounds.

Curriculum objectives

- To use further prefixes and suffixes and understand the guidance for adding them.
- To add suffixes beginning with vowel letters to words ending in 'fer'. (Spelling appendix)

Success criteria

- I can choose the correct spelling for 'fer' words when a suffix is added.

Year 5 Practice Book links:

- (pages 18–19): No stress!

Adding suffixes to words ending 'fer'

Learn

What is the rule for adding suffixes to words ending **fer**?

When adding the suffix **fer**, you double the end consonant if the final vowel is stressed.

You do not double the end consonant if the final vowel is unstressed.

Below are some examples for adding suffixes to words ending in **fer**.

refe**r** + ed = refe**rr**ed
stressed vowel sound   end consonant doubled

transfe**r** + ing = transfe**rr**ing
stressed vowel sound   end consonant doubled

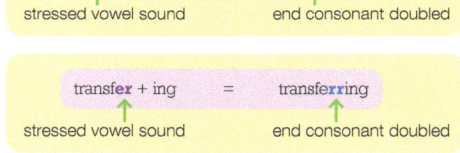

BUT

refe**r** + ence = refe**r**ence
unstressed vowel sound   end consonant **not** doubled

Activities

1. Write the correct ending for each root word.
   a. refer + ing   refering
                           referring
   b. transfer + ed   transferred
                           transfered
   c. refer + e   refere
                           referee
   d. prefer + ence   preferrence
                           preference
   e. prefer + ing   preferring
                           prefering

28 Vocabulary

---

34   Year 5 Vocabulary

'ie' or 'ei'?

Prior learning

- Know that the /ee/ and /ay/ sounds can be spelled in different ways.

Learn

- Use flash cards with 'ie' and 'ei' words on them. Either hold them up for the whole class to read in unison or ask for hands up.
- Produce a set of cards for groups to work with. Provide as many different words as possible containing 'ie' and 'ei'. Ask the children to group them together in ways that make sense. Encourage them to say the words out loud.

Curriculum objectives

- To spell words with the /ee/ sound spelled 'ei' after 'c'. (Spelling appendix)

Success criteria

- I am more confident when spelling words with 'ie' or 'ei' in them.

100 English Lessons Year 5 links:

- Starter activity 4 (page 12): Spelling words with 'ei' for /ee/ after 'c'
- Autumn 2, Week 4 (page 62): Lesson 5, Words with 'ei' after 'c'
- Autumn 2, Assess and review (page 69): Words with 'ei' for /ee/ after 'c'

Year 5 Practice Book links:

- (pages 22–23): Except after 'c'

Activities

- Use the activities in the textbook and on pages 22–23 of the *Year 5 Practice Book* to consolidate understanding.

Write

- Challenge the children to use the words in a piece of writing such as an opening of a story or a letter. It could be very silly. For instance, 'Dear Mr Field, I am writing to express my grief over the height your trees have achieved. Having received complaints from other neighbours…'
- Give out squared paper and ask pairs to create a word search puzzle containing five 'ie' and five 'ei' words. Make it harder by having diagonal words, words spelled backwards and by filling in the spare squares with random 'ie' and 'ei' letters. Note down the words to find. Ask them to swap with another pair.

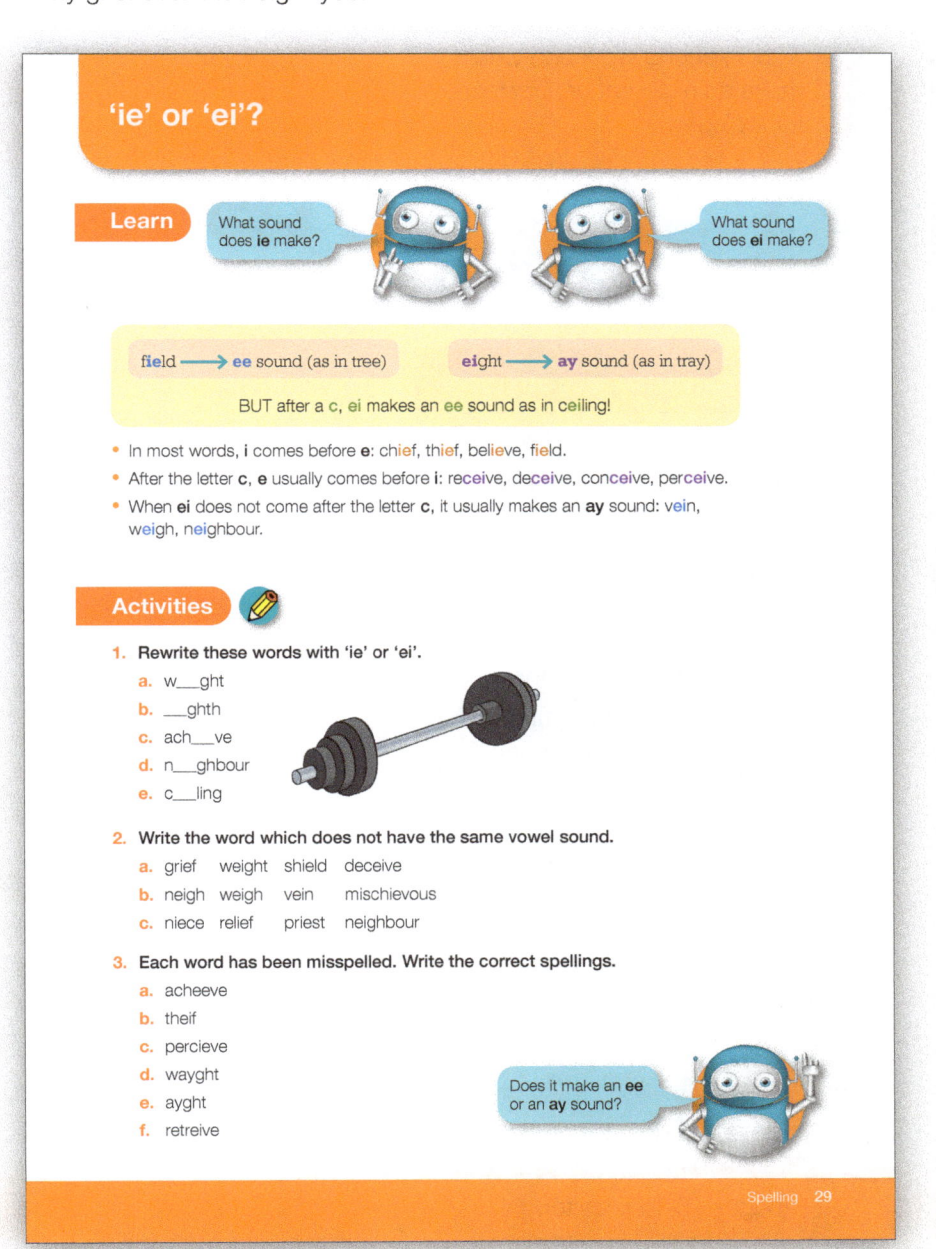

'ie' or 'ei'?

Learn

What sound does **ie** make? What sound does **ei** make?

f**ie**ld → **ee** sound (as in tree)   **ei**ght → **ay** sound (as in tray)

BUT after a **c**, **ei** makes an **ee** sound as in c**ei**ling!

- In most words, **i** comes before **e**: ch**ie**f, th**ie**f, bel**ie**ve, f**ie**ld.
- After the letter **c**, **e** usually comes before **i**: re**cei**ve, de**cei**ve, con**cei**ve, per**cei**ve.
- When **ei** does not come after the letter **c**, it usually makes an **ay** sound: v**ei**n, w**ei**gh, n**ei**ghbour.

Activities

1. Rewrite these words with 'ie' or 'ei'.
   a. w___ght
   b. ___ghth
   c. ach___ve
   d. n___ghbour
   e. c___ling

2. Write the word which does not have the same vowel sound.
   a. grief   weight   shield   deceive
   b. neigh   weigh   vein   mischievous
   c. niece   relief   priest   neighbour

3. Each word has been misspelled. Write the correct spellings.
   a. acheeve
   b. theif
   c. percieve
   d. wayght
   e. ayght
   f. retreive

Does it make an **ee** or an **ay** sound?

Year 5 Spelling

Letter strings: 'ough'

Prior learning

- Understand what 'letter string' means.
- Know that some letter strings can make different sounds in different words.

Learn

- The George Bernard Shaw poem from *Year 5 Practice Book*, page 24, is a good focus for this letter string. Read this poem aloud to the class. It begins with 'ough' spellings, but is brilliant for reading at many other points within spelling work and would make an excellent centrepiece for a display.

Curriculum objectives

- To spell words containing the letter string 'ough'. (Spelling appendix)

Success criteria

- I know how to spell different words with 'ough' in them.
- I know how to pronounce different words with 'ough' in them.

100 English Lessons Year 5 links:

- Spring 1, Assess and review (page 101): Words with '-ough'

Year 5 Practice Book links:

- (pages 24–25): Pronunciation variations
- (pages 26–27): It's tough!

Activities

- Use the activities in the textbook and on pages 24–27 of the *Year 5 Practice Book* to consolidate understanding.
- As an extension to the activities, challenge pairs or threes to come up with rhymes for the six different sounds that 'ough' can make. Can they find rhymes that have the same letter string? Can they also find rhymes that have a different letter string to make the same sound?

Write

- Ask the children to compose a simpler version of the poem in the *Year 5 Practice Book*. They should concentrate only on rhymes that involve words with 'ough' in them. This could be done in pairs or threes, while offering independent working to those who would relish the challenge of having a go entirely on their own.

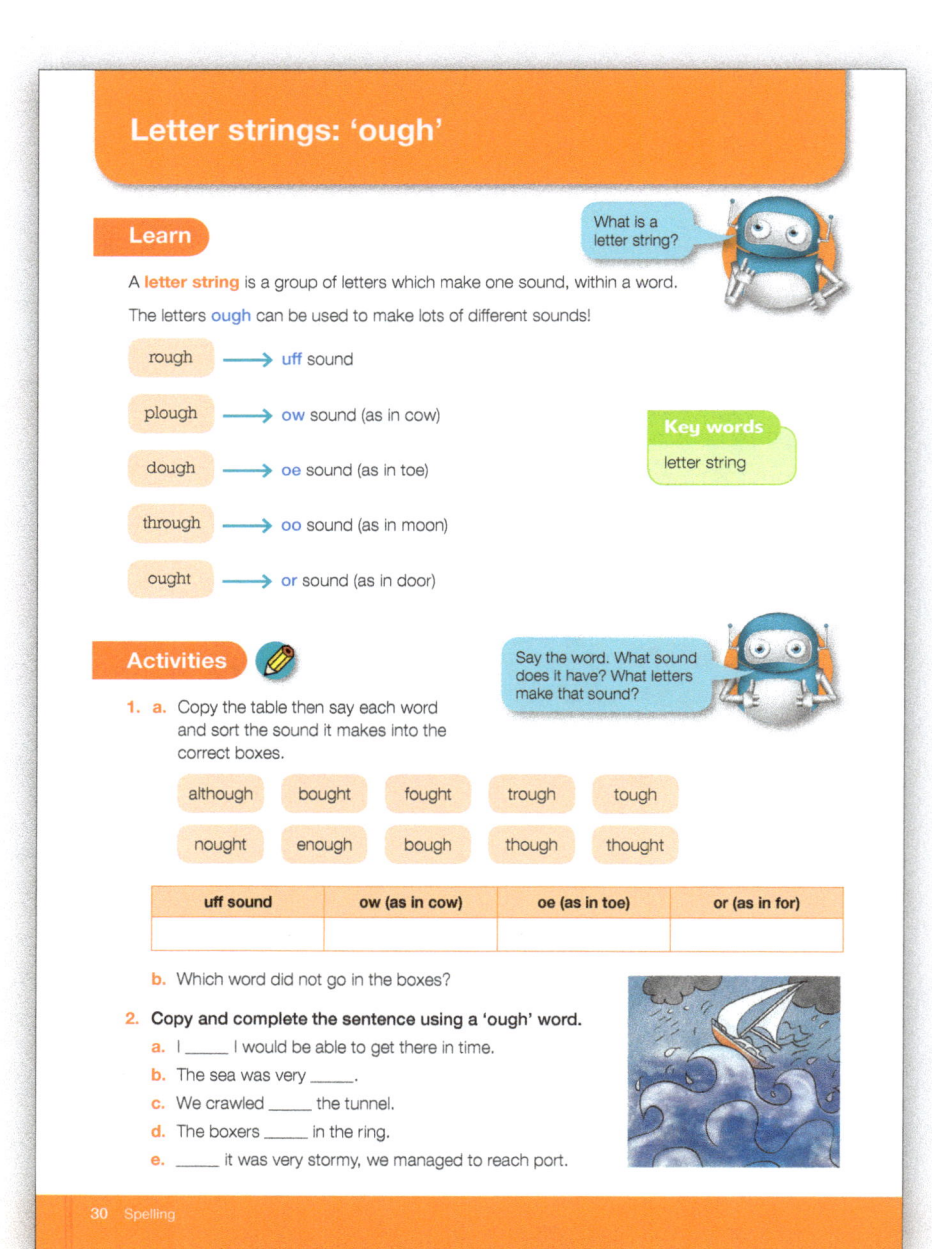

Letter strings: 'ough'

Learn

What is a letter string?

A **letter string** is a group of letters which make one sound, within a word.
The letters **ough** can be used to make lots of different sounds!

- rough → **uff** sound
- plough → **ow** sound (as in cow)
- dough → **oe** sound (as in toe)
- through → **oo** sound (as in moon)
- ought → **or** sound (as in door)

Key words: letter string

Activities

Say the word. What sound does it have? What letters make that sound?

1. a. Copy the table then say each word and sort the sound it makes into the correct boxes.

   although bought fought trough tough
   nought enough bough though thought

uff sound	ow (as in cow)	oe (as in toe)	or (as in for)

   b. Which word did not go in the boxes?

2. Copy and complete the sentence using a 'ough' word.
   a. I _____ I would be able to get there in time.
   b. The sea was very _____.
   c. We crawled _____ the tunnel.
   d. The boxers _____ in the ring.
   e. _____ it was very stormy, we managed to reach port.

Silent letters

Prior learning

- Know that there are a range of words containing silent letters.

Learn

- Hold a discussion to find out how many different words with silent letters are already known to the children. Ask them: *Do you know any words with silent letters in them?* Give them a clue that you've just used one. Give them more clues to others.
- Explain how sometimes you can sound out the silent letter to help remember the spelling, such as in 'lis-ten' or you can use a mnemonic such as 'an island is land'.
- Point out the repeated patterns of 'wr', 'st' and 'kn' in the examples given in the textbook.

Activities

- Use the activities in the textbook and on pages 28–29 of the *Year 5 Practice Book* to consolidate understanding.
- Having completed the *Practice Book* activity, try to use two or three of the words in one sentence.

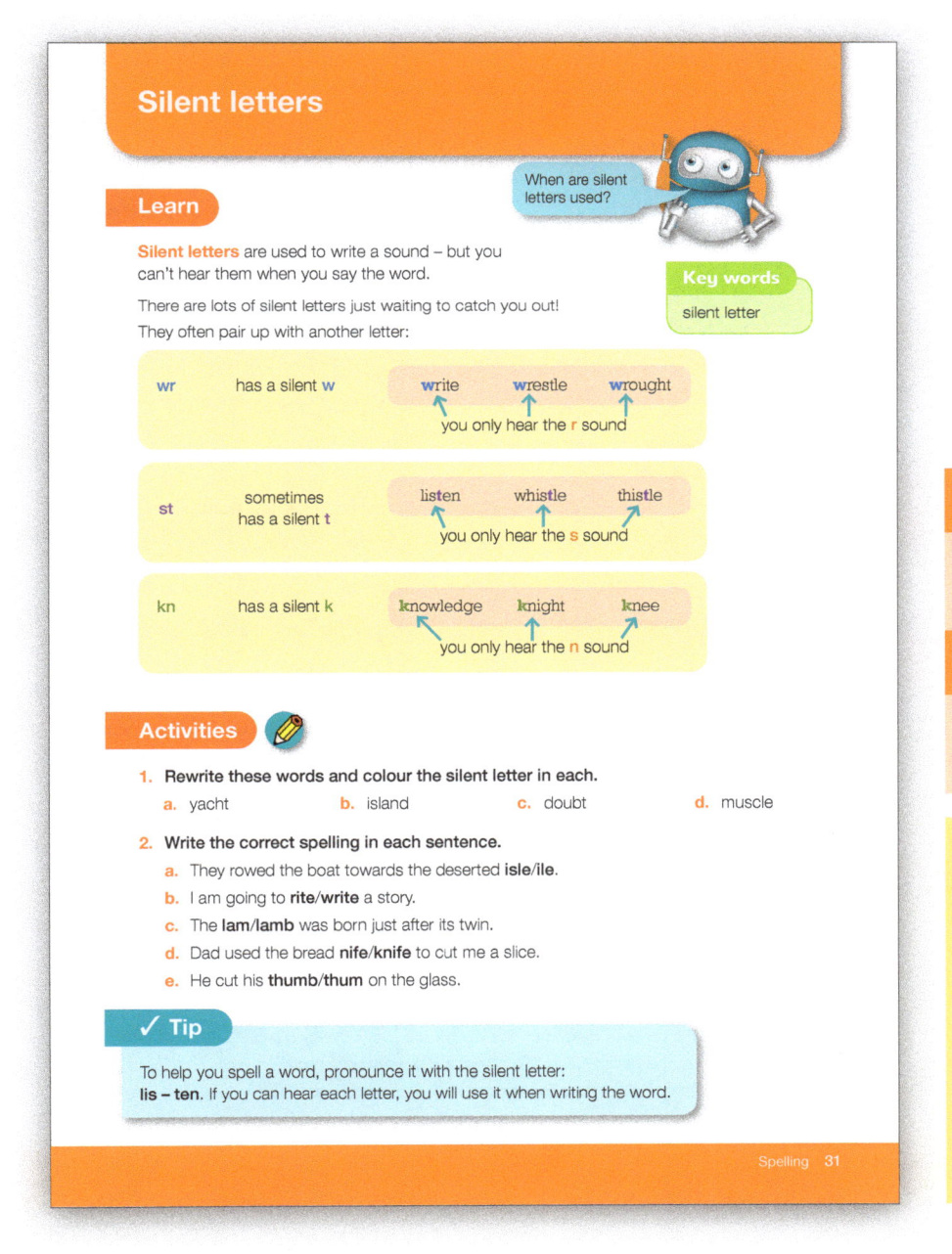

Silent letters

Learn

Silent letters are used to write a sound – but you can't hear them when you say the word.

There are lots of silent letters just waiting to catch you out! They often pair up with another letter:

wr	has a silent w	write wrestle wrought — you only hear the **r** sound
st	sometimes has a silent t	listen whistle thistle — you only hear the **s** sound
kn	has a silent k	knowledge knight knee — you only hear the **n** sound

When are silent letters used?

Key words: silent letter

Activities

1. Rewrite these words and colour the silent letter in each.
   a. yacht   b. island   c. doubt   d. muscle

2. Write the correct spelling in each sentence.
   a. They rowed the boat towards the deserted **isle/ile**.
   b. I am going to **rite/write** a story.
   c. The **lam/lamb** was born just after its twin.
   d. Dad used the bread **nife/knife** to cut me a slice.
   e. He cut his **thumb/thum** on the glass.

✓ Tip

To help you spell a word, pronounce it with the silent letter: **lis – ten**. If you can hear each letter, you will use it when writing the word.

Spelling 31

Curriculum objectives

- To spell some words with 'silent' letters.

Success criteria

- I can spell some new words with silent letters.

100 English Lessons Year 5 links:

- Autumn 1, Week 1 (page 21): Lesson 5, Silent letters
- Summer 2, Week 2 (page 184): Lesson 5, Silent letters

Year 5 Practice Book links:

- (pages 28–29): Shhh...

Words ending 'cious' and 'tious'

Prior learning

- Know that there is a range of words taking the suffix 'ous'.

Learn

- Explain to the children that this is a difficult set of spellings that don't properly follow easy rules. Tell them that if they can pair up the new spelling with shorter words that contain the same root, this will give them a good chance of remembering.
- The lessons in *100 English Lessons Year 5* will also help to give children more practice with these spellings.

- Ask them to take a look at the examples in the textbook and see if they can apply any previous knowledge to help with the words in activity 1, for instance 'ferocious' from 'ferocity'.

Talk

- As a class, how many of the words can you put into context in a short phrase or sentence? Next, see if anyone can put any of the words into a two-word phrase which they will act out at the front, but the trick is to use the same opening letter of the extra word to echo the 't' or 'c' of the key spelling. For instance, a 'ferocious cat'.

Activities

- Use the activities in the textbook and on pages 6–7 of the *Year 5 Practice Book*.
- Ask the children to write five sentences containing one of the new spellings.

Curriculum objectives

- To spell endings which sound like /shus/ spelled 'cious' or 'tious'. (Spelling appendix)

Success criteria

- I can spell a range of words ending with the letter strings 'cious' and 'tious'.

100 English Lessons Year 5 links:

- Autumn 1, Week 1 (page 21): Lesson 4, Adjectives ending with /shus/
- Summer 1, Week 4 (page 158): Lesson 5, Words ending /shus/

Year 5 Practice Book links:

- (pages 6–7): Delicious and nutritious!

Words ending 'cious' and 'tious'

Learn

How can we spell the sound /**shus**/?

When a word ends with the sound /**shus**/ it can be spelled **cious** (as in deli**cious**) or **tious** (as in cau**tious**).
In these words the /**sh**/ sound is spelled **ci** or **ti**.
Sometimes the spelling of a root word helps us, for example: grace → gracious
space → spacious   infect → infectious   caution → cautious
ambition → ambitious. However, most of the time we just have to learn them!

Activities

1. Sort out these words into two sets: words spelled 'cious' and words spelled 'tious'.

   ferocious   ambitious   gracious   infectious   spacious   fictitious
   vicious   atrocious   superstitious   fractious   precious
   suspicious   nutritious   cautious   delicious   scrumptious

2. Make up a silly sentence for each of these cluster of words. Use your sentences to remember the spelling pattern in the future.
   a. vicious, atrocious, ferocious, suspicious   c. ambitious, cautious, infectious, fractious
   b. precious, delicious, spacious, gracious   d. nutritious, fictitious, superstitious, scrumptious

3. Write out each sentence and choose a word from the box to complete the sentence.

   infectious   ferocious   nutritious   superstitious   scrumptious

   a. The chocolate cake with sprinkles on it was completely _____.
   b. The tennis player had a _____ snack of nuts and banana before the match.
   c. When Abdul had chickenpox he had to stay away from school because he was _____.
   d. My _____ aunt is frightened of black cats.

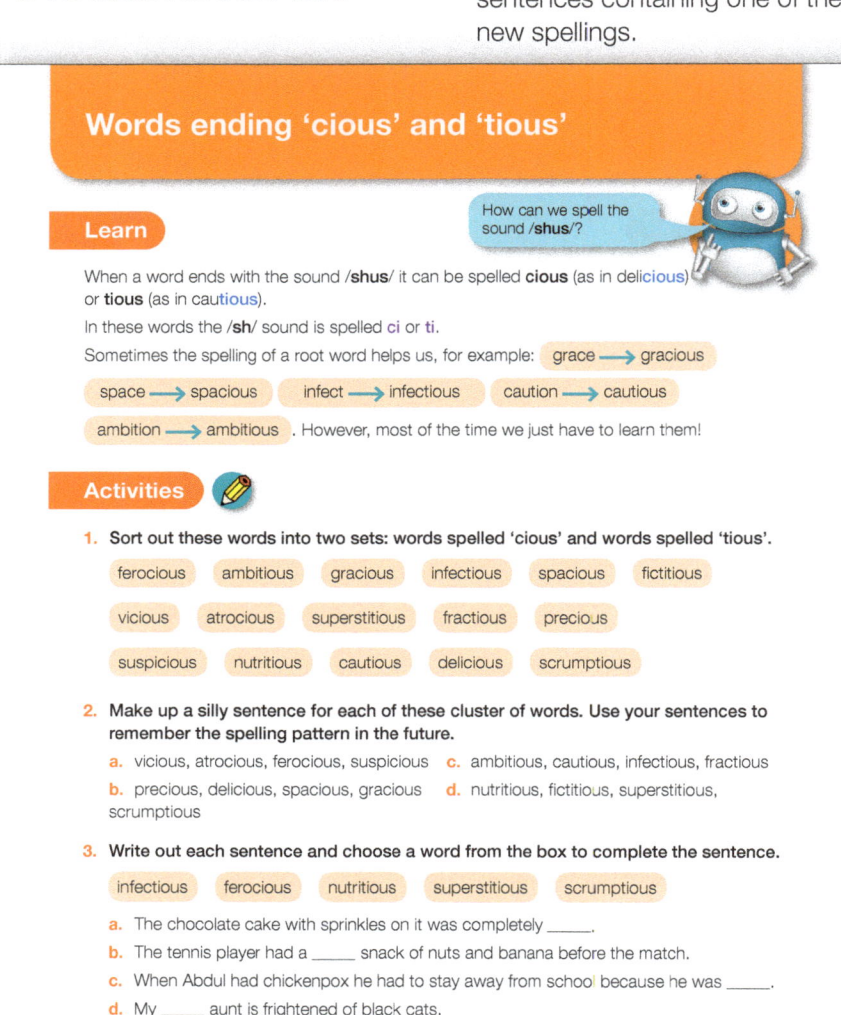

4. Write the word, completing it with 'ci' or 'ti'.
   a. The princess cried when she lost her pre___ous diamond ring.
   b. My little cousin Oscar is very frac___ous when he is hungry.
   c. Scarlet was jealous of her sister's spa___ous new room.
   d. The movie star was very gra___ous when the girls asked for her autograph.

Words ending 'cial' or 'tial'

Prior learning

- Know that 'c' and 't' can be combined with 'ious' to make the /sh/ sound.

Learn

- Point out how there are similarities to the spellings of 'cious' and 'tious' words. We can think of how the root word might be spelled to help us with 'cial' and 'tial' too.
- Together, look at the tip in the textbook and try some examples.

Activities

- Use the activities in the textbook and on pages 8–9 of the *Year 5 Practice Book*.
- Ask the children to complete activity 1 in pairs, then reinforce the learning by writing the matches on the board as a class.
- Point out the infuriating words 'spatial' and 'beneficial' which do not follow the root word rule. Tell the children that English spelling is so beautifully unique that there are some spellings that just have to be learned as individuals!

Words ending 'cial' or 'tial'

Learn

How can we spell the /shul/ sound?

When words end in the /shul/ sound, the ending can be spelled **cial** (as in spe**cial**) or **tial** (as in par**tial**). The /**sh**/ sound in these words is spelled **ci** or **ti**.

Activities

1. Can you pair up these words? Write the matching words together.

A	B
president	torrential
office	presidential
race	artificial
commerce	commercial
part	confidential
crux	crucial
face	facial
torrent	official
artifice	racial
confident	partial

    ✓ **Tip**

    We can often work out if the word is spelled **cial** or **tial** by remembering the spelling of the root word, for example:
    part → partial and race → racial.

    ⚠ Beware of the exceptions:
    space → spatial; benefit → beneficial

2. Write each of the sentences and add the missing word from the box below.

    | residential | beneficial | initial | preferential | sequential | superficial |

    a. Most sportsmen find it _____ to warm up before exercising.
    b. The children in Year 5 are going on a _____ course for a week.
    c. Fabio programmed the robot to perform a number of _____ movements.
    d. The doctor said that Abi's cut was _____ and only needed a plaster.
    e. My first _____ is T (for Tamsin).
    f. Toby gets _____ treatment because he is the son of the headmaster.

3. Choose 'ci' or 'ti' to complete these words. Write each sentence and include the correct spelling for the incomplete word.

    a. Josh's little brother, Alfie, is our unoffi___al team mascot.
    b. Lucky Kuba has a substan___al amount of Lego.
    c. It is antiso___al to play your music too loud – it's also bad for your ears!
    d. My father, who is a spy, reads many confiden___al documents.
    e. It is essen___al, but very hard, to get a good night's sleep before an exam.
    f. Aikedo, Tae Kwon Do, Kung Fu and Karate are all mar___al arts.

Spelling 33

Curriculum objectives

- To spell endings which sound like /shul/. (Spelling appendix)

Success criteria

- I can spell some new words ending in 'cial' or 'tial'.

Year 5 Practice Book links:

- (pages 8–9): Special and essential

Year 5 Spelling 39

Relative clauses

Prior learning

- Know what relative clauses and relative pronouns do.

Learn

- Recap relative clauses and pronouns from Year 5 (see pages 18–19 of this book).
- Find a few novel openings that contain relative clauses. Read aloud to the class, missing out the relative pronoun and asking them which word should fill the gap. To begin with, do this with no clues, then when a pronoun is correctly spotted, write it on the board until you have all six – 'who', 'which', 'where', 'when', 'whose' and 'that'.
- If the chosen extracts also contain sentences with implied relative pronouns, extend the learning to this once they have grasped the idea of spotting relative pronouns. Perhaps also suggest redrafting the author's sentences to support this learning.

Activities

- Use the activities in the textbook and on pages 64–65 of the *Year 6 Practice Book* to consolidate understanding.
- Extend the textbook activity by asking the children to take any of the sentences on the page and create a follow-on sentence that also contains a relative clause. Support this follow-up by preparing suitable sentences on cards which are sliced into three and mixed up.

Relative clauses

Learn

What is a relative clause?

A **relative clause** is a type of subordinate clause that adds information about a previous noun.

Relative clauses start with a **relative pronoun**.

| that | which | who | whom | whose | where | when |

Relative pronouns introduce a relative clause and are used to start a description about a noun.

The **man**, **whose car it was**, shouted angrily.

Relative clause, starts with **whose**.
Describes what the **man** owned. It modifies the noun.

Key words
relative clause
relative pronoun

The **lioness**, **which was only two years old**, was used to being with people.

Relative clause, starts with **which**.
Describes the **lioness**. It describes the noun.

Relative clauses are often enclosed by commas. They start with a relative pronoun.

Activities

1. Write a relative clause for these sentences.
   a. The hotel, ____, was next to the beach.
   b. August, ____, is very busy.

2. Copy the table. Then put a tick to show the type of clause for the words in bold.

Sentence	Main clause	Subordinate clause	Relative clause
a. The rain, **which fell heavily**, made us cancel the trip.			
b. We called at Jacob's house **after we had seen Josh**.			
c. Unless you are able to pay tomorrow, **the trip will be full**.			

Grammatical words 9

Curriculum objectives

- To use relative clauses beginning with 'who', 'which', 'where', 'when', 'whose', 'that' or with an implied (omitted) relative pronoun.

Success criteria

- I can identify and use relative pronouns.
- I can identify and create relative clauses.

100 English Lessons Year 6 links:

- Summer 1, Week 3 (pages 153–155): Lesson 2, Being an editor; Lesson 5, Relative clauses
- Summer 1, Assess and review (page 165): Relative clauses

Year 6 Practice Book links:

- (pages 64–65): Everything's relative

Year 6 Grammatical words

Modal verbs and Adverbs of possibility

Prior learning

- Know that modal verbs and adverbs of possibility tell you how certain things are.

Learn

- Ask the children to name any modal verbs that they can. Develop a list on the board. Provide a sentence and change the modal verb each time to explore the effect. For example:
  - I can juggle.
  - I would juggle if I had something to juggle with.
  - I could juggle some cups in the staffroom.
  - I may do some juggling in tomorrow's lesson.

- Also review adverbs of possibility, which also do a similar job. For example:
  - Maybe I will learn to juggle.
  - I will definitely learn to juggle.
- Explore how likely each modal verb is, use the diagram in the textbook to support this.

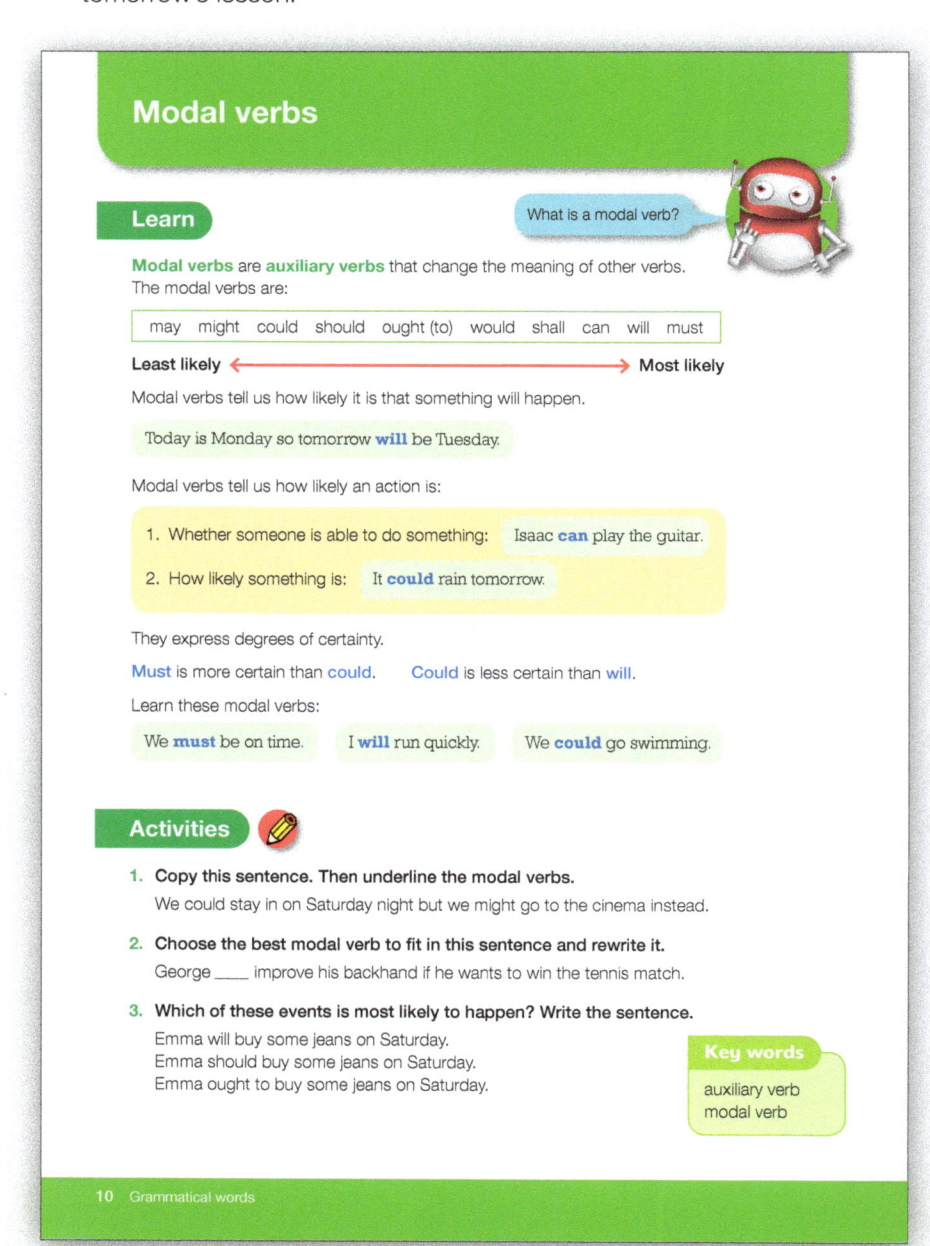

Curriculum objectives

- To use modal verbs or adverbs to indicate degrees of possibility.

Success criteria

- I can use different modal verbs and adverbs of possibility.
- I can understand how they can change the meaning of a sentence.

Modal verbs

Learn — What is a modal verb?

Modal verbs are **auxiliary verbs** that change the meaning of other verbs. The modal verbs are:

| may | might | could | should | ought (to) | would | shall | can | will | must |

Least likely ←—————————————————→ Most likely

Modal verbs tell us how likely it is that something will happen.

Today is Monday so tomorrow **will** be Tuesday.

Modal verbs tell us how likely an action is:

1. Whether someone is able to do something: Isaac **can** play the guitar.
2. How likely something is: It **could** rain tomorrow.

They express degrees of certainty.
Must is more certain than **could**. **Could** is less certain than **will**.
Learn these modal verbs:

We **must** be on time. I **will** run quickly. We **could** go swimming.

Activities

1. Copy this sentence. Then underline the modal verbs.
   We could stay in on Saturday night but we might go to the cinema instead.

2. Choose the best modal verb to fit in this sentence and rewrite it.
   George ____ improve his backhand if he wants to win the tennis match.

3. Which of these events is most likely to happen? Write the sentence.
   Emma will buy some jeans on Saturday.
   Emma should buy some jeans on Saturday.
   Emma ought to buy some jeans on Saturday.

Key words

auxiliary verb
modal verb

10 Grammatical words

Talk

- Prepare a series of topic cards for the children, and a set of modal verb and adverb of possibility cards. Ask the children to choose a topic card and modal verb/adverb card and to combine them to make a statement.
- Keep the same topic card and choose a different modal verb/adverb card and revise the statement. Ask the children to explain the difference between the two statements.

Activities

- Use the activities in the textbook and on pages 60–61 of the *Year 6 Practice Book* to consolidate understanding.
- As an extension, ask the children to write the opening of a story that contains as many as possible of the modal verbs and adverbs of possibility which have been used in the activities.

Write

- Working with a partner, ask the children to write a script, choosing what levels of possibility and certainty they are going to put across between someone who is in a position of power and someone who ought to obey that power. It could be: a teacher and a child; a parent and child; a police officer and a member of the public; a doctor and a patient; a head teacher and a member of staff; a boss and a worker.
- Ask them to experiment with modal verbs and adverbs of possibility – perhaps the power is strongly in one direction; perhaps the weaker character grows stronger; perhaps both characters are very certain about what they want. Ask confident pairs to perform and use this as the basis for further discussion.

Adverbs of possibility

Learn

What is an adverb of possibility?

An adverb of possibility shows how certain we are about something.

These adverbs of possibility show we are sure of something happening.

definitely   certainly   obviously   clearly

These adverbs of possibility show we are less sure of something happening.

probably   perhaps   maybe   possibly

Maybe and **perhaps** usually come at the **beginning** of a sentence or clause.

Perhaps there will be ice cream for tea.
Maybe I can have a tablet for my birthday.

Other adverbs of possibility usually come in front of the main verb.

It is **clearly** going to rain.

However, they come after the verbs **am**, **is**, **are**, **was** and **were**.

It is **certainly** a busy road.

Activities

1. Choose the best adverb of possibility for each sentence.
   a. It is ____ six miles to town.
   b. I can ____ come to see you later.
   c. ____ we can have tea together?

2. Explain how each adverb of possibility changes the meaning of the sentences below.
   - We are clearly going to win this game.
   - We are possibly going to win this game.

Grammatical words 11

100 English Lessons Year 6 links:

- Summer 1, Week 3 (page 155): Lesson 4, Modal verbs
- Summer 2, Week 2 (pages 182–184): write a report using *Street Child*
- Summer 2, Week 3 (pages 185–187): compose a newspaper article about the life of a Victorian child

Year 6 Practice Book links:

- (pages 60–61): School rules OK!

Subjects and objects

Prior learning

- Know what nouns, pronouns and verbs are.

Learn

- Introduce the terms 'subject' and 'object' to the children. Give examples using physical objects. For example: 'Mrs Thomas is holding a pen'. 'Mrs Thomas' is the subject and 'a pen' is the object.
- However, ensure the children understand that the 'object' of the sentence is who or what is having the verb done to it and could be another person, 'Mrs Thomas is pointing at James' – in this example, 'James' is the object.

- Tell the children that many sentences in all types of text will have a subject and an object. Demonstrate this by opening a variety of books at random pages and reading extracts aloud. Identify the subjects and objects, showing the children how often sentences do contain both.
- Note, the concept of 'subject' and 'object' is closely linked to active and passive sentences see pages 96–97 of this book.

Talk

- Arrange a table of random objects and ask for volunteers to come to the front. Tell them that you have a table of objects, which are going to become the objects of sentences. The volunteers are willing subjects who are also going to be the subjects of the sentences. The children then offer sentences which contain a subject and object.
- Demonstrate an example: 'The teacher throws the orange up and down.'

Curriculum objectives

- To know and use the terminology 'subject' and 'object'. (Grammar appendix)

Success criteria

- I can identify the subject and object in a sentence I read.
- I can write sentences with subjects and objects.

Subjects and objects

Learn

What are subjects and objects?

Every sentence has a **subject**.
The subject is the person or thing that does the action of the verb.

Many sentences have **objects** as well. The object has the action of the verb done to it. Objects are usually nouns, pronouns or noun phrases.

Let's look at an example.

I am selling.

This sentence has a subject but not an object. The verb is selling. **I** am doing the selling, so **I** is the **subject**.

I am selling **my bike**.

In this sentence **I** am still doing the selling, so **I** is still the **subject**. My bike is being sold. **My bike** is having the action of the verb done to it, so **my bike** is the **object**.

In a sentence:
- subjects usually come before the verb
- objects usually come after the verb.

Key words

subject
object

12 Grammatical words

94 Year 6 Grammatical words

- Give the activity a greater element of drama by asking for suggestions where the volunteers have to play a role. For example: 'The very angry boxer picks up the pen.'
- Each time a sentence is offered and acted, point out the subject and object for reinforcement.

Activities

- Use the activities in the textbook and on pages 123–125 of the *Year 6 Practice Book* to consolidate understanding.
- As an extension activity, ask the children to create a set of their own sentences, all with a subject and object. Ask them to underline or mark the subjects and objects they use to show that they know which is which.

Write

- Write a rhyming poem where each line runs subject – verb – object. Tell the children that the poem does not have to make perfect sense.

Activities

1. Rewrite the sentence then circle the subject in each of them.
    a. My mum drove the car.
    b. Our cat ate its food.

2. Write the object in each of these sentences.
    a. Dad is making tea.
    b. The dog chased the cat.

3. Write the subjects and objects in each of these sentences.
    a. You can ride your bike to school.
    b. Sadie sells shoes.
    c. Ronny, who is older than me, rides his motorbike to work.
    d. Mrs Burman, a very strict head teacher, runs her school well.

4. Write these sentences with your own subjects and objects.
    a. [Subject] threw the ball to [object].
    b. [Subject] scored three [object].
    c. [Subject] who lives at the end of our street, owns [object].
    d. [Subject], my best friend, sings [object].

Remember, subjects usually come before the verb. Objects usually come after the verb.

Grammatical words 13

Year 6 Practice Book links:

- (pages 123–125): All in agreement

Year 6 Grammatical words 95

Active and passive verbs

Prior learning

- Understand and identify subject and object within sentences.

Learn

- Recap what a subject and object is. Explain that most sentences have a subject and object and we call these active sentences – the object is having the verb done to it – but sometimes we want to use a different form.
- Using your own actions at the front of the class, demonstrate how to change verbs from active to passive. For example:
  - I am writing on the board. / The board is being written on by me.
- I just read a paragraph aloud. / The paragraph was read aloud by the teacher.
- Explain how the passive is formed, use the textbook to support this.
- Next, invite volunteers to try out an action, which they then vocalise in both its active and passive forms.

Active and passive verbs

Learn

What are active and passive verbs?

Active and **passive verbs** are different forms of verbs.

Most sentences use the active form of a verb. This means that the subject is doing the action and the object has the action done to it.

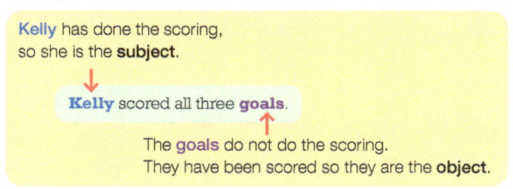

Kelly has done the scoring, so she is the **subject**.

Kelly scored all three **goals**.

The **goals** do not do the scoring. They have been scored so they are the **object**.

When the **passive** is used, the object moves to the front and becomes the subject. The original subject moves to the end of the sentence but does not become the object. It becomes part of a **prepositional phrase** (you add 'by'). You also change the verb by adding 'was' or 'were'.

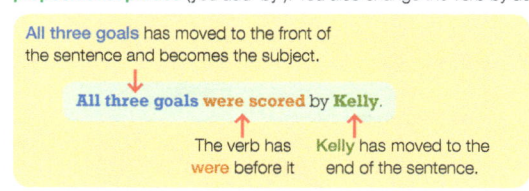

All three goals has moved to the front of the sentence and becomes the subject.

All three goals **were scored** by Kelly.

The verb has **were** before it. Kelly has moved to the end of the sentence.

The passive form can be used in formal writing.

To recognise the passive, look at the end of the sentence. It usually has **by** someone or something after the verb.

Key words
active verb
passive verb
prepositional phrase

14 Grammatical words

Curriculum objectives

- To use passive verbs to affect the presentation of information in a sentence.

Success criteria

- I can use the passive form of verbs.

96 Year 6 Grammatical words

Talk

- Ask the children to work in pairs to invent simple sentences with active verbs which they then transform to the passive.

Activities

- Use the activities in the textbook and on pages 62–63 of the *Year 6 Practice Book* to consolidate understanding.
- Support the learning with a set of cards with simple sentences on them. Some should be active, some passive. In pairs, ask the children to sort them into two columns. Once they have split the cards into active and passive, challenge them to pick active sentences to transform into passive and vice versa.

Write

- To consolidate the learning with some practice, ask the children to create a formal report about something they have done recently. They should try to use the passive voice as often as possible.

100 English Lessons Year 6 links:

- Starter activity 8 (page 12): Active to passive, passive to active
- Autumn 2, Week 2 (pages 54–56): use *Alice in Wonderland* to create formal court language
- Autumn 2, Assess and review (page 69): The passive verb form and the subjunctive verb form
- Spring 1, Week 2 (page 88): Lesson 5, Formal speech
- Spring 1, Week 4 (pages 92–94): write a letter from an evacuee
- Spring 2, Week 2 (page 119): Lesson 3, The Kling Kling Bird
- Summer 1, Week 1 (pages 147–149): write a poster based on *Carrie's War*
- Summer 1, Week 3 (pages 153–155): use the passive voice to act as an editor
- Summer 2, Weeks 2 and 3 (pages 182–187): write formal accounts based on *Street Child*
- Summer 2, Week 5 (page 192): Lesson 3, Non-fiction features

Year 6 Practice Book links:

- (pages 62–63): Active and passive

Activities

1. **Rewrite these sentences in the passive form.**
   a. The chef made a wonderful meal.
   b. The police officer arrested the criminal.
   c. A mechanic mended our car.
   d. My cousin sent a letter to the Pope.
   e. Four mums from Yorkshire rowed a boat across the Atlantic Ocean in 2016.

2. **Rewrite these sentences in the active form. Take care to make sure the subject and verb agree.**
   a. A good time was had by everyone.
   b. The world record was smashed by the runner.
   c. Terrible floods have been caused by torrential rain.
   d. Many homes have been destroyed in America by a massive hurricane.
   e. Our cat was rescued from a tree by the fire brigade.

3. **Read the following sentences with a partner. Decide whether each sentence is active or passive.**
   a. The winning shot was made by Alisha.
   b. Our team won the league.
   c. Small mammals are hunted by eagles.
   d. Many people have climbed Mount Everest.
   e. The bird ate the worm.

The subjunctive

Prior learning

- Know that speech and writing can be either formal or informal.

Learn

- Introduce this topic using *100 English Lessons Year 6* Starter activity 14. Use also the information in the textbook.
- Explain that the subjunctive form of verbs is very helpful in formal speech or writing, particularly when you want to stress urgency or importance.

Talk

- Have a game of 'Subjunctivitis'.
- The idea is for an imaginative class discussion where every statement begins with the subjunctive form being used. For example:
  - If I were very rich…
  - If I were the prime minister…
  - If I were to rule the world…
  - If I were to leave school right at this moment…

Curriculum objectives

- To recognise vocabulary and structures that are appropriate for formal speech and writing, including subjunctive forms.
- To know the difference between structures typical of informal speech and structures appropriate for formal speech and writing. (Grammar appendix)

Success criteria

- I can recognise subjunctive forms and understand the subtle differences in meaning.

The subjunctive

Learn

What is the subjunctive?

The **subjunctive** is a form of the verb used in formal speech or writing.

The subjunctive uses only the simple form of a verb. For example, the simple form of **to run** is **run**.

The word **that** will help you to recognise the subjunctive. If the verb can be followed by **that** and something **should** happen, you will be using the subjunctive:

I demand that you be quiet.

Subjunctives are used in different ways.

• **verb + that**	to advise that to ask that to command that to demand that to insist that to propose that to recommend that to request that to suggest that
• **after phrases + that**	it is essential that it is desirable that it is vital that
• **I, he or she + were**	It is more natural to write **if I was** to go to, but this would be informal. The subjunctive form would be **if I were** to go to. This is known as the past subjective.
• **verb + that + be**	I insist that you be here.

- When these verbs are followed by **that**:

  to advise   to propose   to recommend   to request   to insist   to ask   to command   to suggest

  For example:

  I insist that you be here.

- When these phrases are followed by **that**:

  it is essential   it is desirable   it is vital

  For example:

  It is essential that you be on time tonight.

Subjunctives are only used in formal speech or writing. They are often used to suggest urgency or importance.

16 Grammatical words

98 Year 6 Grammatical words

Activities

- Use the activities in the textbook and on pages 58–59 of the *Year 6 Practice Book* to consolidate understanding.
- As an extension, ask the children to rewrite one or two sentences from the activities using a different verb form. Next, try to explain the subtle difference in meaning when the subjunctive form is used.

Write

- Pretending to be the head teacher, write a formal letter which explains the school rules to prospective parents. Use the subjunctive form as often as possible.
- Write a poem where every line begins with the words 'If I were…'

Activities

1. Rewrite these sentences, adding the subjunctive form of the verb in each sentence.
   a. It is important that you **be/are** on time for the show.
   b. If I **was/were** you, I would take the risk.

2. Find and copy the subjunctive in these sentences.
   a. If I were to give you £25, what would you do with it?
   b. The teacher asked that her students be quieter.

3. Rewrite these sentences in a formal style, using subjunctives.
   a. If Zoe was to play instead of Zena, we'd win easily tonight.
   b. It is important that you are here on time.
   c. I wish it was Saturday.
   d. If only my car was more reliable.
   e. It is essential that pupils are polite.
   f. I advise that you are present at the hearing.
   g. Dr Lazarus asked that the patient waits outside.
   h. Chaz requested that Ziggy came to his party.
   i. It is essential that the referee is allowed to control the game.

Key words
subjunctive

100 English Lessons Year 6 links:

- Starter activity 14 (page 13): Subjunctive forms
- Autumn 2, Week 2 (page 56): Lesson 5, Guilty or innocent?
- Autumn 2, Assess and review (page 69): The passive verb form and the subjunctive verb form
- Spring 1, Week 2 (page 88): Lesson 5, Formal speech
- Summer 1, Week 1 (pages 147–149): design a poster
- Summer 2, Week 3 (pages 185–187): write a newspaper article
- Summer 2, Week 5 (pages 191–193): write a biographical account of Brunel's life

Year 6 Practice Book links:

- (pages 58–59): Seriously subjunctive

Commas to clarify meaning

Prior learning

- Understand the basic building blocks of simple sentences.

Learn

- Find a text with complex sentences, containing plenty of commas. Read the text aloud to the class in a monotone, only taking a breath at full stops. Ask them what is wrong. If they reply that it's boring or you're reading it too fast, prompt them further by saying you are deliberately using the same tone and reading fast because you are missing something out. Once it is established that you have dispensed with the commas, begin the rest of the work.

- Prepare a range of texts from which the commas have been removed. Ask pairs or individuals to put them back in to aid clarity. For differentiation, consider not only length of text, but length of sentences within the text. Provide factual texts as well as fiction.

Activities

- Challenge the children to write pairs of fairly simple sentences where a missing comma or two could completely change the meaning. Advise them to model their creations on sentences from the exercises, but also invite them to create totally new ones.

- Explain that in speech, we can use intonation and pausing to make our meaning clear. Invite confident pairs to the front to act out mini-scenes – perhaps using freeze-frames – to show the difference a comma can make. For example, 'Let's eat, Dad!' is very different to 'Let's eat Dad!'

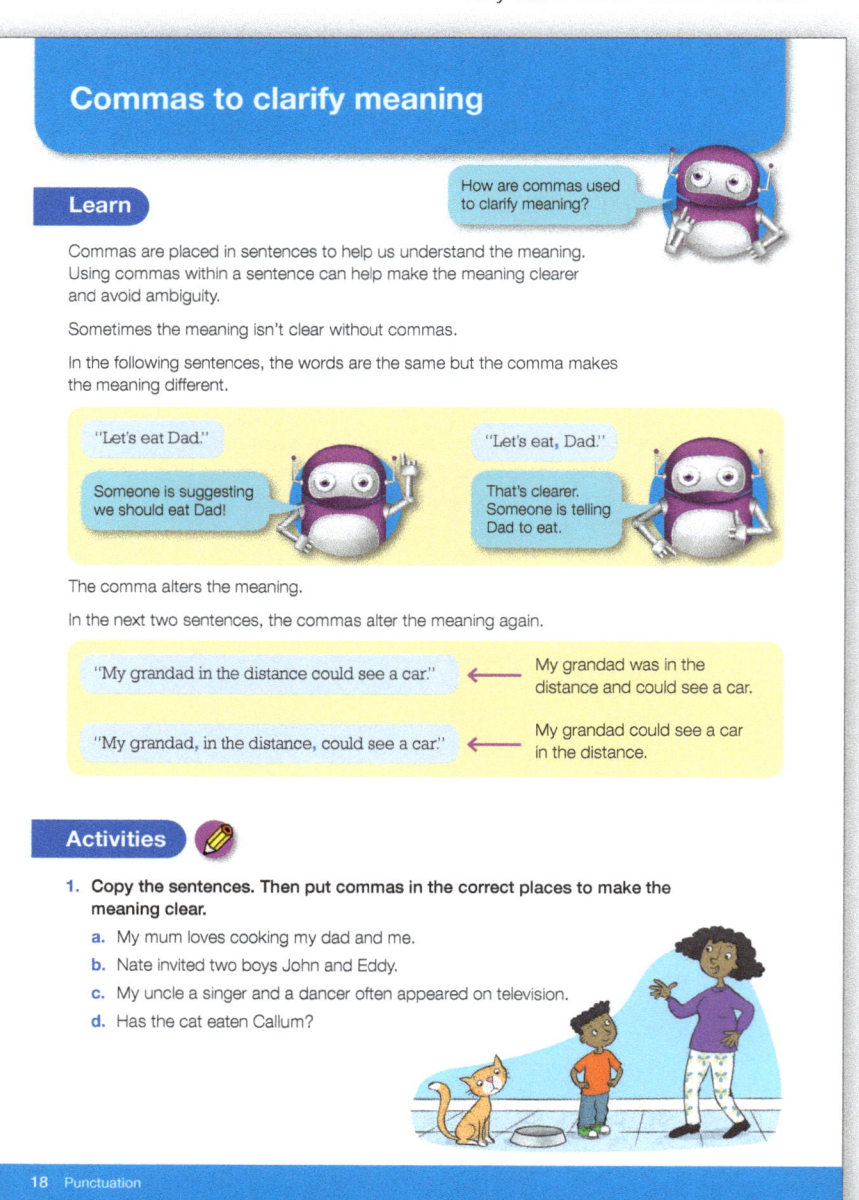

Curriculum objectives

- To use commas to clarify meaning or avoid ambiguity in writing.

Success criteria

- I can use commas within a sentence to clarify meaning.

100 English Lessons Year 6 links:

- Spring 2, Week 3 (page 123): Lesson 4, Plan and draft
- Summer 1, Week 3 (page 154): Lesson 2, Being an editor
- Summer 2, Week 5 (page 192): Lesson 2, Isambard Kingdom Brunel

Year 6 Practice Book links:

- (pages 75–76): Commas to the rescue!

Commas to clarify meaning

Learn

How are commas used to clarify meaning?

Commas are placed in sentences to help us understand the meaning. Using commas within a sentence can help make the meaning clearer and avoid ambiguity.

Sometimes the meaning isn't clear without commas.

In the following sentences, the words are the same but the comma makes the meaning different.

"Let's eat Dad." — Someone is suggesting we should eat Dad!

"Let's eat, Dad." — That's clearer. Someone is telling Dad to eat.

The comma alters the meaning.

In the next two sentences, the commas alter the meaning again.

"My grandad in the distance could see a car." ← My grandad was in the distance and could see a car.

"My grandad, in the distance, could see a car." ← My grandad could see a car in the distance.

Activities

1. Copy the sentences. Then put commas in the correct places to make the meaning clear.
   a. My mum loves cooking my dad and me.
   b. Nate invited two boys John and Eddy.
   c. My uncle a singer and a dancer often appeared on television.
   d. Has the cat eaten Callum?

Question tags

Prior learning

- Know that a question can be used for the purpose of persuasion.

Learn

- Write on the whiteboard: 'Question tags are very easy to spot and also easy to use.' Explain to the children that this is a statement with which they will soon agree.
- Edit the sentence on the board, changing the full stop to a comma and adding '…aren't they?', underlining your addition. Tell the children that you have tagged the words '…aren't they?' onto the end of the statement and turned it into a question.
- Say to them: *The part I've tagged on is a question tag. Question tags are very easy to spot and use, aren't they?*
- Once they are nodding in agreement, feed them some statements and ask volunteers to add a question tag.
- Point out that question tags can be very useful in persuading others of your point of view.

Activities

- Perhaps using some of the class ideas from your introduction, ask the children to write ten sentences which contain question tags.
- Start by saying: *So, you're going to write ten sentences with question tags in them, aren't you? There you go, that's your first one, isn't it? Oh, there's another one!*

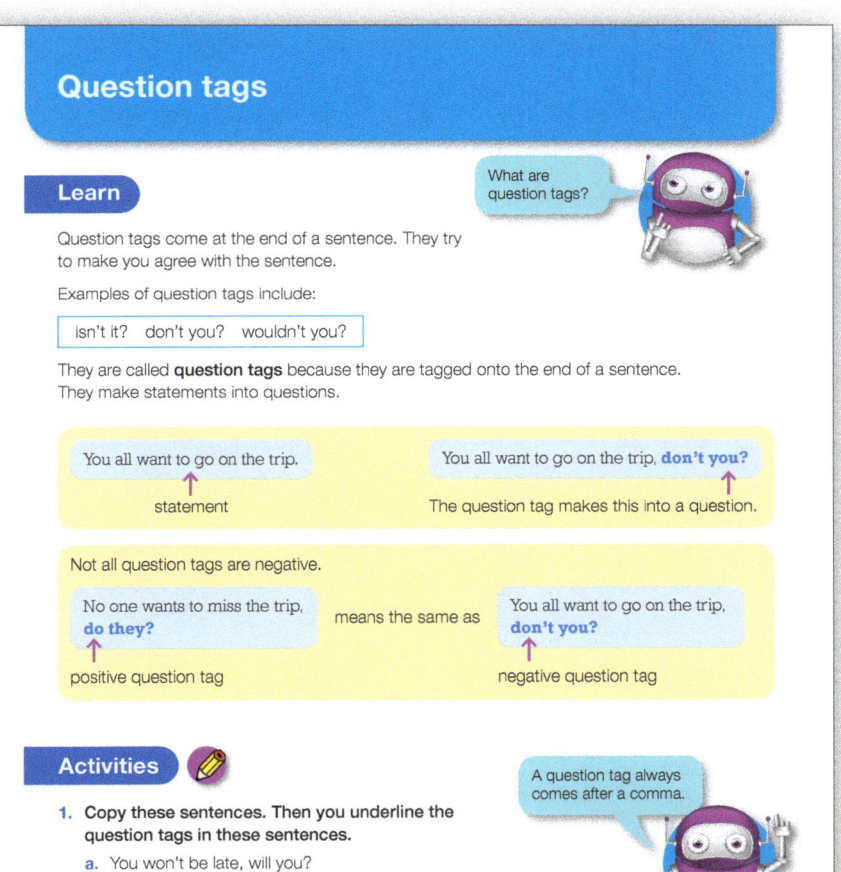

Question tags

Learn

What are question tags?

Question tags come at the end of a sentence. They try to make you agree with the sentence.

Examples of question tags include:

isn't it?   don't you?   wouldn't you?

They are called **question tags** because they are tagged onto the end of a sentence. They make statements into questions.

You all want to go on the trip.
↑
statement

You all want to go on the trip, **don't you?**
↑
The question tag makes this into a question.

Not all question tags are negative.

No one wants to miss the trip, **do they?**   means the same as   You all want to go on the trip, **don't you?**
↑   ↑
positive question tag   negative question tag

Activities

A question tag always comes after a comma.

1. Copy these sentences. Then you underline the question tags in these sentences.
   a. You won't be late, will you?
   b. We're going to the cinema, aren't we?

2. Add appropriate question tags to these sentences.
   a. You'd like pizza for tea, ____?
   b. This is the right answer, ____?

Question tags are easy, aren't they?

Punctuation 19

Curriculum objectives

- To know the difference between structures typical of informal speech and structures appropriate for formal speech and writing (for example, the use of question tags: 'He's your friend, isn't he?'). (Grammar appendix)

Success criteria

- I can use question tags in my speech and writing.

100 English Lessons Year 6 links:

- Summer 1, Week 1 (page 148): Lesson 3, Question tags
- Summer 2, Week 1 (page 181): Lesson 4, Informal dialogue
- Summer 2, Week 4 (pages 188–190): write a street child story

Year 6 Punctuation   101

Hyphens

Prior learning

- Know that hyphens can be used to add prefixes.
- Understand that hyphens can help clarify meaning.

Learn

- Remind children of the work they did in Year 5 (see pages 24–25 of this book) that hyphens are very useful for joining words together and clarifying meaning.
- Recap when hyphens are used: when a prefix ends with the same vowel as at the beginning of the root word and to join two words that are acting as one word.
- Spend time reviewing different examples and looking at the effect with and without hyphens. Use the examples from the textbook or Starter activity 19 from *100 English Lessons Year 6* to support this.

Activities

- Use the activities in the textbook and on pages 20–21 and 83 of the *Year 6 Practice Book* to consolidate understanding.
- Ask the children to look at writing they have done recently and see whether they need any hyphens for clarity.
- Take a look at how creative compound adjectives can be in the hands of great writers like Shakespeare or Dickens – and it's all down to the humble hyphen.

Curriculum objectives

- To use hyphens to avoid ambiguity.

Success criteria

- I can use hyphens in different ways to make the meaning clear.

100 English Lessons Year 6 links:

- Starter activity 19 (page 15): Hyphens
- Spring 2, Week 3 (page 123): Lesson 4, Plan and draft
- Summer 1, Week 3 (page 154): Lesson 2, Being an editor
- Summer 2, Week 1 (page 181): Lesson 4, Informal dialogue
- Summer 2, Assess and review (page 197): Hyphens

Year 6 Practice Book links:

- (pages 20–21): Do you need a hyphen?
- (page 83): Warning! Man eating crocodile

Hyphens

Learn

What is a hyphen?

Hyphens are punctuation marks that are used to:
- join words together
- clarify meaning
- help pronunciation
- follow some prefixes.

Sometimes we join words together using a hyphen to show that they are linked.

> It was a **low-budget** film.

In this sentence, the film is neither **low** nor **budget**. We have to link the two words together to get **low-budget**, meaning it did not cost much.

The meaning of some sentences isn't clear without a hyphen.

> Joe Montana was a famous American football player.

The sentence is ambiguous. Was Joe a famous American who played football, or was he famous for playing American football? Adding a hyphen shows that Joe played American football.

> Joe Montana was a famous **American-football** player.

Without a hyphen, we would not know how to pronounce words like **re-enter**. The hyphen tells us that the letters on either side of it are both pronounced.

Here are some examples of when hyphens follow prefixes.

ex-police officer   **all**-inclusive   **self**-conscious

Key words
hyphen

Activities

1. Copy the sentences. Then insert hyphens to join the correct words together.
   My mother in law is coming for Sunday lunch.

2. Copy the sentences. Then insert a hyphen to make it clear that the instruments have not been used much.
   My uncle, a retired surgeon, showed me some of his little used instruments.

3. Rewrite 'resign' with a hyphen to show that it means 'to sign again'.

Bullet points

Prior learning

- Identify the use of bullet points in non-fiction texts.

Learn

- Recap on the work on bullet points the children did in Year 5 (see page 27 of this book).
- Use find examples of books, articles or web pages using bullet points. Take a look at whether the writers have been consistent in their usage. Did they use a colon? Did they use all capitals or all small letters for the first letter of each point? Did they only use a full stop for the last point?

Activities

- As an extension activity, ask the children to invent their own shop or business, realistic or fantasy and to write a bullet-pointed list to show at least five features.

Curriculum objectives

- To punctuate bullet points consistently.

Success criteria

- I can use a colon to introduce bullet points.
- I can choose either upper or lower case for the first letter of each item.
- I can punctuate the list correctly.

100 English Lessons Year 6 links:

- Autumn 1, Week 2 (pages 22–24): write a leaflet about Brazil
- Autumn 1, Assess and review (page 37): Punctuating bullet points
- Spring 1, Week 2 (pages 86–88): create a guide to magical creatures
- Spring 2, Week 1 (pages 115–117): write an introduction to Africa
- Spring 2, Week 3 (pages 121–123): compose a biographical article about Nelson Mandela
- Summer 2, Week 4 (page 188): Lesson 1, Jim's story
- Summer 2, Week 5 (pages 191–193): compile an account of Brunel's life

Year 6 Practice Book links:

- (pages 84–85): Bullet points

Year 6 Punctuation

Colons and semi-colons in lists

Prior learning

- Know how to use a colon in simple lists and bullet-pointing.

Learn

- Recap the word done in Year 5 on using colons to introduce a list (see page 26 of this book). Practice writing simple lists and asking the children to insert a colon.
- Introduce more complicated lists where one list item contains main words including commas and/or conjunctions. Ask whether it is clear where each item starts and finishes. Introduce a semi-colon and explain how to use it.
- Use starter activity 18 from *100 English Lessons Year 6* to support this.
- Explain that using colons with semi-colons to create a list has similarities to bullet-point usage. The decision as to which to use will depend on the type of text and the length of the list. Sometimes only commas will be needed to separate the items in the list, but when it's more complicated, semi-colons are used for separation.

Activities

- Use the activities in the textbook and on pages 81–82 of the *Year 6 Practice Book* to consolidate understanding.
- Ask the children to create their own lists using colons and semi-colons. For variation, suggest that they do at least one simple list which uses commas for separation and one more

Curriculum objectives

- To use a colon to introduce a list.
- To use a colon to introduce a list and semi-colons within lists. (Grammar appendix)

Success criteria

- I can use colons and semi-colons successfully to punctuate lists.

Colons and semi-colons in lists

Learn

How do you use colons and semi-colons in lists?

Colons introduce lists.

> To build this model tree you will need: glue, scissors, a ruler, tissue paper and some wire.

Semi-colons separate complicated items within a list.

> I had to buy a large loaf from the bakery; cheese and tomatoes from the deli; some onions, carrots and potatoes from the grocer; and some plastic plates from the hardware shop.

Key words
- colon
- semi-colon

Activities

1. Copy these sentences. Then insert colons in the correct places.
   a. You will need to bring with you your passport, plane tickets, money, sun cream and sunglasses.
   b. We now know some countries that border the Mediterranean Sea Egypt, France, Spain and Italy.
   c. Warm waters can be found in the Mediterranean Sea, the Caribbean Sea and the Indian Ocean.

✓ Tip
Remember, the colon is a link. It goes before the items in the list. Sometimes a semi-colon will be used when the items in a list already contain a comma.

2. Rewrite this bullet-pointed list as a sentence.
   I need to go to:
   - the supermarket for dog, cat and fish food
   - the heel bar to get my shoes, boots and sandals mended
   - the library to get some books for my history project.

✓ Tip
Sometimes semi-colons are links as well: they go between the items in a complicated list.

complicated list which uses semi-colons to make the items clear.

- If preparation time allows, create a set of cards for an imaginary house, having, for example, five rooms and twenty-five items. The children then work in groups to decide which items are going into which rooms, and then they write out the contents using colons and semi-colons.

Write

- Set a challenge for writing a story which includes the use of colons and semi-colons in its opening description of the main character approaching a strange house.
- Write three paragraphs: one describing the street; one describing coming through the gate and walking through the garden; one describing moving inside the house and into its rooms.

- Stress that while using the target punctuation is important, it is also important not to overdo it and for the story to have a flow to it.

---

3. Rewrite these passages with colons in the correct places:

   a. The manager looked around the dressing room and said, "Some of you were useless last week, so for this week the defence will be Smith, Brown, Martin, Culshaw and Blair. In midfield I'm having Middleton, Sutton, Mason, Devlin. Up front it will be Nagla and Hussain."

   b. To succeed in life you need a lot of things talent, determination, hard work and a lot of luck.

4. Rewrite these lists with semi-colons in the right places.

   a. I have been learning Spanish on the internet for three weeks. Already I can: tell people my name book a room order drinks at the bar and explain that I do not understand a word they are saying.

   Remember the semi-colon before and *in the last item in the list.*

   b. I have bought all of the birthday presents for my family early this year. For my sister I have a camera and a memory card a box of expensive chocolates and a day at a spa. My mother is getting an imitation diamond necklace two tickets to the cinema, so she can take me as well and some chocolates. My brother is getting nothing because he is always mean to me never does his share of the washing up and plays Taylor Swift at full volume while I am trying to watch television.

5. Rewrite these passages with colons and semi-colons. Gaps have been left to show you where they should go.

   a. The head teacher looked at the boy and said, "Let's have a look at your attendance record. This is what you have done this week   Monday   morning   absent   afternoon late. Tuesday   late in the morning   absent in the afternoon. Wednesday   absent morning   absent afternoon. Need I go on?"

   b. "From now on it's going to be like this   you will attend school every day   be on time   and make sure you are wearing your full uniform. Is that too much to ask?"

Punctuation 23

100 English Lessons Year 6 links:

- Starter activity 18 (page 14): Lists
- Autumn 2, Week 1 (page 53): Lesson 4, Eat me; drink me
- Autumn 2, Week 6 (page 67): Lesson 2, Synopsis
- Spring 1, Week 2 (pages 86–88): create a guide to magical creatures
- Summer 1, Week 3 (page 154): Lesson 3, Why were children evacuated?

Year 6 Practice Book links:

- (pages 81–82): Note what follows

Year 6 Punctuation   105

Separating independent clauses

Prior learning

- Know how semi-colons and colons are used for listing.

Learn

- Tell the class that as well as using colons and semi-colons for separating items in a list, they can be used when separating independent clauses.
- Remind the children that an independent clause can stand alone as a complete sentence and that it will contain a subject and a verb.
- Review the examples in the textbook. You may wish to spend time focusing on one piece of punctuation at a time.
- This is an area that is likely to need a lot of practice and revising. Take opportunities to review examples in class reading and class work.
- Use starter activity 16 in *100 English Lessons Year 6* to support this.

Curriculum objectives

- To use semi-colons, colons or dashes to mark boundaries between independent clauses.

Success criteria

- I can decide which punctuation to use in order to separate independent clauses.

Separating independent clauses

Learn

How do we separate independent clauses?

An independent clause needs a verb and a subject and can stand alone as a complete sentence. Some sentences have more than one independent clause. These can be joined together by colons, semi-colons or dashes.

Colons introduce a second clause that gives more detail to a first one. It shows there is a clear link between the two clauses but gives more emphasis to the second one.

> Mason was worried about asking Della out: he had struggled all day to find the right words.

Semi-colons link clauses of equal strength or importance.

> Tomorrow will be Friday; the day afterwards will be Saturday.

Dashes work like colons but are used in less formal writing.

> Your hair is so long it's getting in your eyes – it could do with cutting.

Activities

1. Rewrite these sentences, combining each pair into one sentence with a colon in the right place.
    a. Full marks in the test again. Just what I expected.
    b. Paris is a beautiful city. You can see many famous sights there.
    c. Martin didn't want to sell his car. He needed the money he would get for it.
    d. The sky looks dark. It will rain heavily all day.
    e. I love Skiathos. I am really looking forward to going there on holiday again.

2. Add an independent clause to complete each one.
    a. I know exactly what I want for my birthday:
    b. We are learning sign language at school:
    c. My brother is getting married next year:
    d. Before I tasted my soup I wondered if I had put too much salt in it:
    e. This year's school production is 'Oliver':

Key words

colon
semi-colon
dash

✓ Tip

Remember colons are used when the second clause tells you more about the first one.

Talk

- As an alternative to completing the activities in writing, work through them with the class on the whiteboard. After each answer is established, ask volunteers for an explanation as to why a particular piece of punctuation is correct in each case.

Activities

- Use the activities in the textbook and on pages 77–78 of the *Year 6 Practice Book* to consolidate understanding.
- As an extension to the activities, ask the children to create some sentences of their own, using the different types of target punctuation and also writing an explanation as to why each choice is the correct one.

---

3. Each of the following sentences has a star that should be a colon or a semi-colon to link independent clauses. Rewrite them with the correct piece of punctuation in place.
    a. My homework is due in tomorrow ★ I'll have to make sure I do it tonight.
    b. I was ten last year ★ this year I'll be eleven.
    c. I didn't do well in the spelling test this morning ★ there were some difficult words in it.
    d. Who dares wins ★ who doesn't dare loses.
    e. America is in the west ★ Russia is in the east.

4. Pick two of your answers and explain why you used a colon in one and a semi-colon in the other.

5. Why is the colon used in the sentence below?
    Two minutes of extra time to go and the score is 0–0: if someone doesn't score soon, we'll be going to penalties.

6. Rewrite the following sentences correctly by inserting either semi-colons or dashes. Compare your answers with a partner and discuss the reasons for them.
    a. Watch what you're doing ★ you could have had my eye out!
    b. The postman has just delivered a parcel I ordered ★ I was expecting it.
    c. Don't put it there ★ put it there!
    d. There is a really interesting programme about China on television tonight ★ it is the kind of thing I like to watch.
    e. All of my friends have phones ★ everybody uses them.

7. Which of these sentences is correct? Compare your answer with a partner. Write an explanation for your choice.
    a. The road is – difficult it's almost impassable – you'll need a strong vehicle.
    b. The road is difficult it's almost – impassable – you'll need a strong vehicle.
    c. The road is difficult – it's almost impassable – you'll need a strong vehicle.
    d. The road is difficult it's – almost impassable – you'll need a strong vehicle.

Punctuation 25

---

100 English Lessons Year 6 links:

- Starter activity 16 (page 14): Semicolon, colon and dash to separate independent clauses
- Autumn 2, Week 1 (page 52): Lesson 3, Alice and the Pigeon
- Autumn 2, Week 5 (pages 63–65): write a playscript
- Autumn 2, Assess and review (page 71): Rules and poems
- Spring 1, Week 2 (pages 86–88): compare two texts
- Spring 1, Assess and review (page 101): Semicolons, colons and dashes
- Spring 2, Week 2 (page 119): Lesson 3, 'The Kling Kling Bird'
- Spring 2, Week 3 (page 122): Lesson 2, Being an editor
- Summer 1, Week 3 (pages 153–155): act as an editor to write an article on the Blitz
- Summer 2, Week 1 (pages 179–181): write a note of advice

Year 6 Practice Book links:

- (pages 77–78): Punctuating clauses

Year 6 Punctuation

Parenthesis

Prior learning

- Understand usage of relative pronouns and relative clauses.
- Know that parenthesis is additional information in a sentence contained in punctuation.

Learn

- Recap the learning from Year 5 (see pages 22–23 of this book). Ask the children to recall what we call extra information in a sentence and which punctuation marks we can use for this.
- Look at the textbook. Point out that the example uses 'which is in Paris' as parenthesis. Challenge the class to recall what kind of pronoun and clause is being used. Once the relative pronouns have been recalled – 'who', 'which', 'where', 'when', 'whose' and 'that' – ask if anyone can think of a different parenthesis using either the same relative pronoun or a different one. For example, 'The Eiffel Tower, when you climb it, is a very tall building' or 'The Eiffel Tower, whose top nearly touches the sky, is a very tall building.' (See page 91 of this book for more on relative clauses.)

Curriculum objectives

- To use brackets, dashes or commas to indicate parenthesis.

Success criteria

- I can use parenthesis, employing brackets, commas or dashes.

Parenthesis

Learn

What is parenthesis?

Parenthesis is the term used for a word, clause or phrase that is inserted into a sentence to provide more detail.
- **Parenthesis** is what is written inside **brackets**.
- **Commas** and **dashes** can do the same job as brackets.

Parenthesis does not make any difference to the understanding of the original sentence. It just gives the reader more information.

The following sentence gives a piece of information.

> The Eiffel Tower is a very tall building.

By adding parenthesis, more detail is given but the meaning remains the same.

> The Eiffel Tower (which is in Paris) is a very tall building.
> parenthesis with brackets

Commas and pairs of dashes can do the same job as brackets.

> The Eiffel Tower, which is in Paris, is a very tall building.
> parenthesis with commas

Dashes tend to be used in less formal writing, such as in an email.

> The Eiffel Tower – which is in Paris – is a very tall building.
> parenthesis with dashes

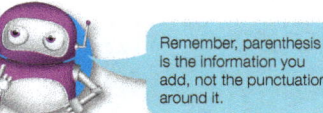

Remember, parenthesis is the information you add, not the punctuation around it.

Key words
- parenthesis
- brackets
- commas
- dashes

Talk

- Provide a range of short texts taken from fiction or factual books. Ask the children to examine them closely to see how many different uses of parenthesis they can find. Can they find examples which use brackets, commas and dashes? Offer the findings to the class, first reading aloud each whole sentence, then reading it without the parenthesis to confirm that it still makes sense.

Activities

- As an extension activity, ask the children to use the sentences given again, but this time adding in different parentheses, playing around with new possibilities. As they begin to explore, point out that the possibilities are actually endless and can lead to some very imaginative and interesting sentences.

Write

- As a follow-up application of their learning, ask the children to find a paragraph or two from a recent piece of their own work and to add parentheses to make it into a more interesting piece of writing. Remind them not to overdo it as this might make their extract too awkward to read.

Activities

1. a. Rewrite the following sentence, inserting the parenthesis using brackets.

   The three men talked quietly in the corner of the cafe.
   Parenthesis: *they looked like spies to me*

   b. Rewrite the following sentence, inserting the parenthesis using commas.

   Denny is joining the army. **Parenthesis:** *my older brother*

   c. Rewrite the following sentence, inserting the parenthesis using dashes.

   Suki won first prize at the dog show. **Parenthesis:** *a long-haired Alsatian*

   d. Rewrite the following sentence, inserting the parenthesis using either brackets, commas or dashes.

   I had to keep very still while the doctor took my stitches out.
   Parenthesis: *who was very gentle*

   e. Rewrite the following sentence, inserting Parenthesis 1 and Parenthesis 2 into the correct places using dashes and commas.

   The strongest wind ever will hit this country.
   Parenthesis 1: *a massive hurricane*
   Parenthesis 2: *probably on Tuesday next week*

Punctuation 27

100 English Lessons Year 6 links:

- Autumn 2, Week 5 (pages 63–65): write a playscript for *Alice in Wonderland*
- Autumn 2, Assess and review (page 71): Rules and poems
- Spring 1, Week 4 (page 94): Lesson 5, Dear diary
- Spring 1, Assess and review (page 103): Formal, informal and archaic language
- Spring 2, Week 3 (pages 121–123): write a biographical account of Nelson Mandela
- Summer 1, Week 3 (pages 153–155): act as an editor
- Summer 2, Week 5 (pages 191–193): research and write about Isambard Kingdom Brunel

Year 6 Practice Book links:

- (pages 79–80): Parentheses on parade

Suffixes: 'ant' or 'ent'; 'ance' or 'ence'; 'ancy' or 'ency'?

Prior learning

- Know that a suffix is added to the end of a root word.

Learn

- Recap these suffixes and use the textbook to help recall some of the techniques you can use to help you.

- Use the 'hesitant', 'innocent' and 'frequent' groups of words to work through orally, pointing out that once the children know one spelling from each group, they can then work out the rest even if the sound of the others doesn't make it clear. For example, remembering 'hesitation', with its very clear vowel sound, will help in remembering 'hesitant', which is unclear.

Talk

- Ask the children to work in groups to think of other words that use one of these suffixes. For example: arrogant, resident, instance, presidency. Use dictionaries to check the spellings. Discuss whether the words found follow the patterns learned or whether they are irregular.

Curriculum objectives

- To use further prefixes and suffixes and understand the guidance for adding them.
- To spell words ending in 'ant', 'ance'/'ancy', 'ent', 'ence'/'ency'. (Spelling appendix)

Success criteria

- I can apply my knowledge of suffixes to spell new words correctly.

Suffixes: 'ant' or 'ent'; 'ance' or 'ence'; 'ancy' or 'ency'?

Learn

Which suffix should I use?

To work out which **suffix** to use, it helps to know that some of them are related.

Words ending in **ation** often use the **ant**, **ance** or **ancy** suffixes.
Let's look at some:

hesit**ation** → hesit**ant** → hesit**ance** → hesit**ancy**

They all have **a** in the suffix!

Use **ent**, **ence** or **ency** after a **soft c** sound or after **qu**:

inno**cent** → inno**cence**

Both have a **soft c** and end with **ent** or **ence**.

fre**qu**ent → fre**qu**ence → fre**qu**ency

Suffixes follow **qu** and end with **ent**, **ence** or **ency**

Key words

suffix

There are words that don't follow these guidelines, which you need to learn.

For example: independ**ent** assist**ance**

If one of a word's suffixes has an **a** in it, other might: assist**ant** assist**ance**

*Unfortunately, there are lots of words that don't follow these guidelines, and so you need to learn them! For example: independent, assistance. But, if one of a word's suffixes contains an **a**, they all will: assistant, assistance.*

Activities

- Once the textbook activities are complete, extend the learning by asking the children to write the words in context, underlining the target words.
- Provide extracts from some factual books to groups of children. Ask them to look for words which end with 'ant', 'ent', 'ance', 'ence', 'ancy' or 'ency'. Write down the words found. Ask them to work together to discuss whether their findings truly contain suffixes – if they do, they should be able to work out which original word has been modified. They may also find that they have discovered words like 'fancy' and 'tent' which don't fit the pattern and can be discarded for the purposes of their research.

Write

- Ask children to compose the opening of a story which contains as many of their new words as possible. Try not to overdo it as this will make the piece sound odd.

Activities

1. Copy and complete each word choosing the correct suffix

Word beginning	'ent' or 'ant'
observ	
innoc	
toler	
obedi	

2. Write the correct spelling from each pair.
   a. buoyency/buoyancy
   b. hesitency/hesitancy
   c. agency/agancy
   d. accountency/accountancy
   e. consistency/consistancy

3. Write each sentence, choosing the correct spelling to complete it.
   a. The non-**existance/existence** of dodos in Mauritius has long been a cause for regret.
   b. Your help is more of a **hindrance/hindrence**.
   c. Please complete the **relevent/relevant** application form.

4. Use the words below in sentences.

   vacancy   redundant   efficiency   frequence   urgency

5. Find a fiction book. Copy these headings:

   ant   ance   ancy   ence   ence   ency

   How many words from your fiction book can you write under each heading?

100 English Lessons Year 6 links:

- Starter activity 3 (page 11): Word endings

Year 6 Practice Book links:

- (pages 10–13): An importANT differENCE

Prefixes: 're', 'dis' or 'mis'?

Prior learning

- Understand that a prefix is added to the beginning of a root word.

Learn

- Take a close look at any passage of writing as a whole class. To begin with look for all prefixes, then specifically for prefixes that are modifying verbs. Point out how common prefixes are in writing and also point out that the word 'prefix' has even got its own prefix in it!

- Remind the children of how hyphens may be used in some examples of words with prefixes, particularly when the meaning is unclear or the word looks too strange on the page.

Activities

- Use the activities in the textbook and on pages 20–21 and 68–69 of the *Year 6 Practice Book* to consolidate understanding.

- Prepare a range of verbs and ask the children to discuss which prefixes might work to create new words. Which ones are they sure about? Do they know what the meaning is? Encourage them to use a dictionary to check whether they are correct or not. Ask them to feed back their findings to the class.

Curriculum objectives

- To use further prefixes and suffixes and understand the guidance for adding them.
- To apply their growing knowledge of root words, prefixes and suffixes (morphology and etymology), as listed in the Spelling appendix, both to read aloud and to understand the meaning of new words that they meet.

Success criteria

- I can add the correct prefixes to verbs to change their meanings.

Year 6 Practice Book links:

- (pages 20–21): Do you need a hyphen?
- (pages 68–69): Switch the meaning

Prefixes: 're', 'dis' or 'mis'?

Learn

The prefix **re** means again or back. It changes the meaning of the word.

regain — to gain **again**
redo — to do **again**
readjust — to adjust **again**

The prefix **dis** changes the word to its opposite meaning (often means not).

disagree — **not** agree
disinterest — **not** interested
disbelieve — **not** believing

The prefix **mis** also changes the verb to its opposite meaning (often to **do it badly**).

misuse — to use **badly**
mistreat — to treat **badly**
misbehave — to behave **badly**

Activities

1. Copy the lists below and draw lines to match the prefixes to the root words. Then write each new word.

   re   loyal
   dis   judge
   mis   design

2. Copy the table. Then use prefixes to change the meaning of these words so they match their definitions.

Word	New word	Definition
place		to put back again
calculate		to work out wrongly
tasteful		objectionable

Adding suffixes to words ending 'fer'

Prior learning

- Know that some consonants get doubled up when adding certain suffixes.

Learn

- Recap on the learning from Year 5 (see page 34 of this book). Use the example in the textbook to support this.
- Work through several examples together and practise saying words aloud to hear whether the final vowel is stressed or unstressed.

Activities

- Use the activities in the textbook and on pages 18–19 of the *Year 6 Practice Book* to consolidate understanding.
- As an ongoing extension, ask the children to think of other 'fer' words such as 'confer' and 'suffer'. Make a small wall chart to which new finds can be added over time.

Adding suffixes to words ending 'fer'

Learn

How do I add a suffix starting with a vowel to words ending with **fer**?

To add a suffix starting with a vowel to words ending **fer**.
- You double the end consonant if the final vowel is stressed.
- You do not double the end consonant if the final vowel is unstressed.

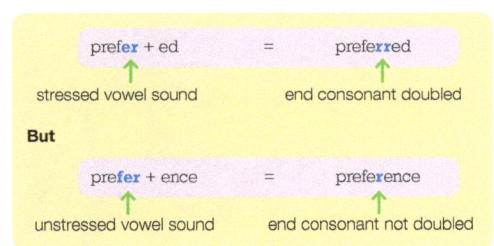

pre**fer** + ed = pref**err**ed
↑ ↑
stressed vowel sound   end consonant doubled

But

pre**fer** + ence = prefe**r**ence
↑ ↑
unstressed vowel sound   end consonant not doubled

Activities

1. Rewrite each sentence, choosing the correct word.
   a. The doctor was refering/referring him to a specialist.
   b. The head teacher wrote a glowing reference/refference.

2. Write each word with the correct ending.
   a. infer — ed / red   infer — ence / rence
   b. differ — ing / ring   differ — ence / rence
   c. transfer — ed / red   transfer — ence / rence

Vocabulary 31

Curriculum objectives

- To add suffixes beginning with vowel letters to words ending in 'fer'. (Spelling appendix)

Success criteria

- I can choose the correct spelling for 'fer' words when a suffix is added.

Year 6 Practice Book links:

- (pages 18–19): Would you prefer a double 'r'?

Year 6 Vocabulary 113

Synonyms and Antonyms

Prior learning

- Know how to use a thesaurus.

Learn

- Introduce and explain the terms 'synonym' and 'antonym' – you may wish to cover these separately.
- Explain that the search for synonyms is particularly useful when redrafting a piece of writing. Tell the children that it can take time, but using a thesaurus will help them to find replacement words which may improve the quality of what has already been written. (See pages 132–133 of this book for more on introducing thesauruses)
- It may be that they will find words which they already know and can instantly slot into their work. But also give a word of warning – if they intend to use an unfamiliar word, always check it in a dictionary first to make sure that its meaning is exactly what's required.

Talk

- Have a game of 'Word tennis' across the class. Set a time limit of around five seconds for each half to 'hit' the 'ball' back across. The ball is hit by giving a correct synonym or antonym to the last word in the 'rally'. The teacher holds a stock of words to begin each rally. Points are scored when the ball is not 'returned' in the time given.
- The activity can also be run across tables or between pairs of children. A set of cards could be made for the 'serving' (starting) word for a rally. The cards might even be marked up as verbs, adverbs or adjectives to further enhance the learning.

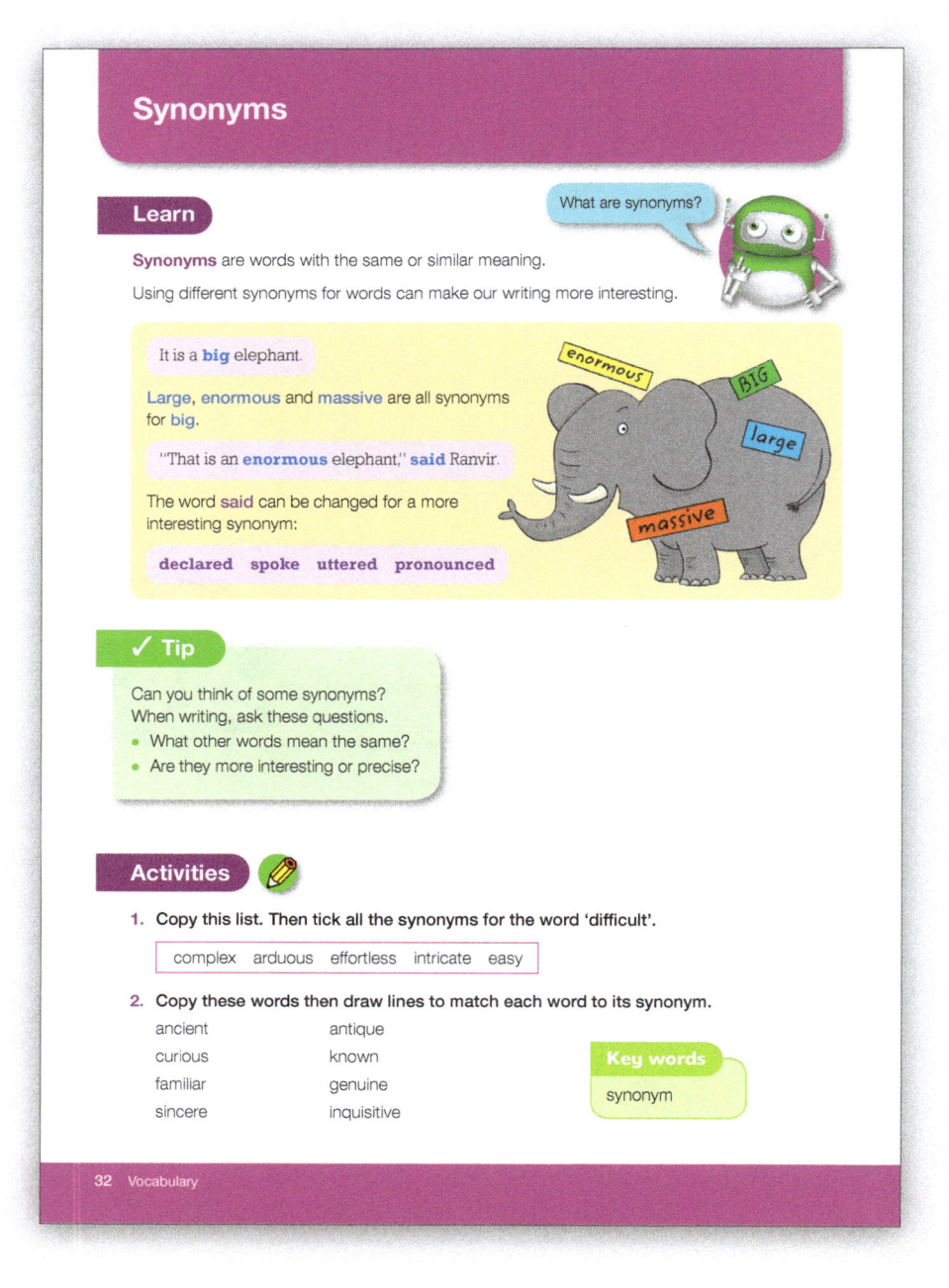

Curriculum objectives

- To understand how words are related by meaning as synonyms and antonyms. (Grammar appendix)

Success criteria

- I can explore for synonyms to make my writing more interesting.
- I know what an antonym is.

Synonyms

Learn

What are synonyms?

Synonyms are words with the same or similar meaning.
Using different synonyms for words can make our writing more interesting.

It is a **big** elephant.

Large, **enormous** and **massive** are all synonyms for **big**.

"That is an **enormous** elephant," **said** Ranvir.

The word **said** can be changed for a more interesting synonym:

declared   spoke   uttered   pronounced

✓ Tip

Can you think of some synonyms? When writing, ask these questions.
- What other words mean the same?
- Are they more interesting or precise?

Activities

1. Copy this list. Then tick all the synonyms for the word 'difficult'.

   complex   arduous   effortless   intricate   easy

2. Copy these words then draw lines to match each word to its synonym.

ancient	antique
curious	known
familiar	genuine
sincere	inquisitive

Key words
synonym

32 Vocabulary

114   Year 6 Vocabulary

Activities

- Use the activities in the textbook and on pages 48–49 of the *Year 6 Practice Book* to consolidate understanding.
- Create some wall charts for commonly used verbs, adjectives and adverbs with suggestions for synonyms and antonyms.

Write

- Thesaurus work: compile a list of common verbs and adjectives which are being regularly used by the children in their writing. Write them on the whiteboard. For example: 'walk', 'run', 'say', 'big', 'small', 'exciting'. Ask them to use thesauruses to find more uncommon words. Once a range of synonyms has been found, ask the children to put them into the context of a sentence. For words which are brand new to them, ask them to double-check the meaning in a dictionary before trying to place the words into context.
- Undertake the same task with a range of adjectives or adverbs focusing this time on antonyms.

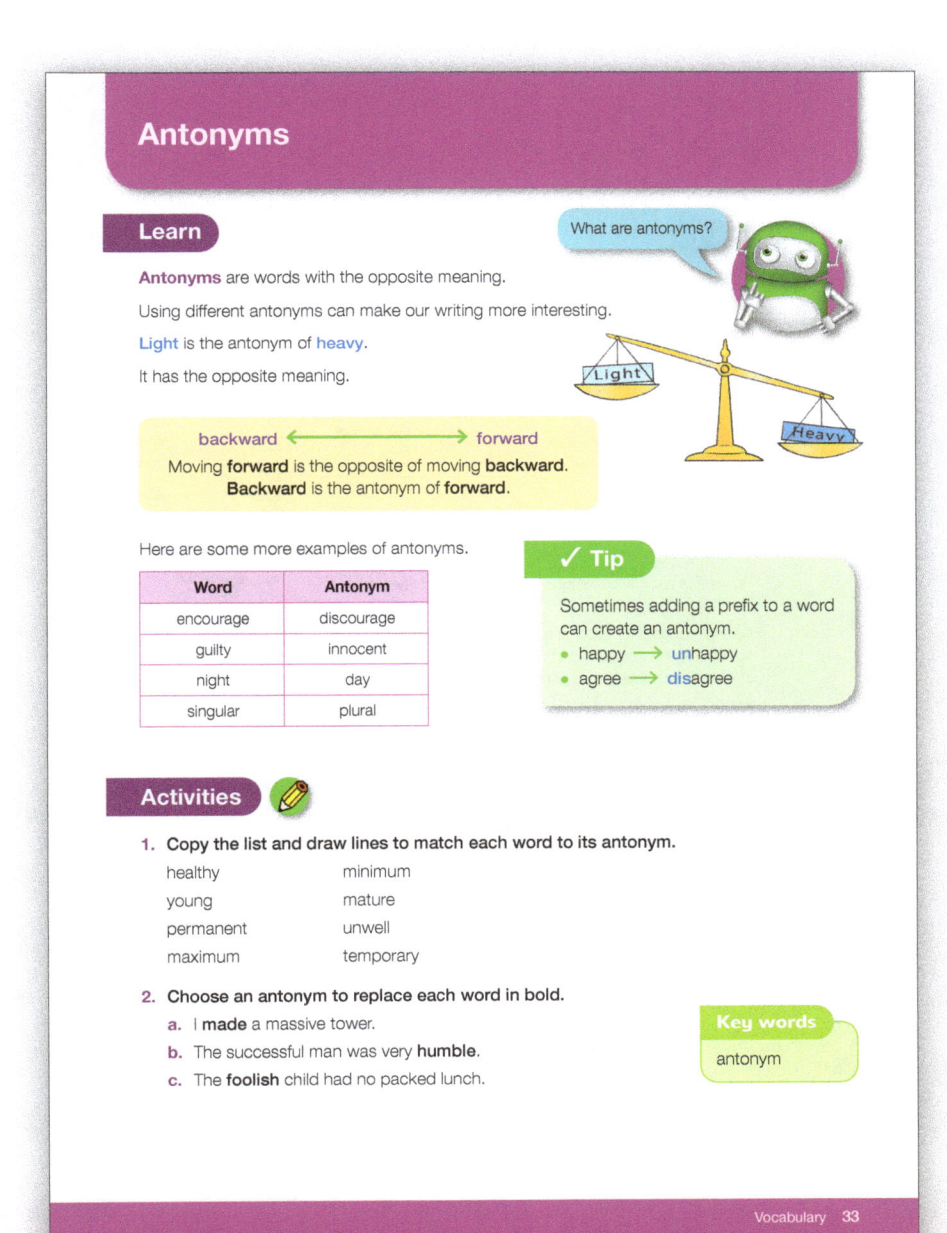

Antonyms

Learn

What are antonyms?

Antonyms are words with the opposite meaning.

Using different antonyms can make our writing more interesting.

Light is the antonym of **heavy**.

It has the opposite meaning.

backward ⟷ forward

Moving **forward** is the opposite of moving **backward**.
Backward is the antonym of **forward**.

Here are some more examples of antonyms.

Word	Antonym
encourage	discourage
guilty	innocent
night	day
singular	plural

✓ Tip

Sometimes adding a prefix to a word can create an antonym.
- happy ⟶ **un**happy
- agree ⟶ **dis**agree

Activities

1. Copy the list and draw lines to match each word to its antonym.

   healthy   minimum
   young   mature
   permanent unwell
   maximum   temporary

2. Choose an antonym to replace each word in bold.
   a. I **made** a massive tower.
   b. The successful man was very **humble**.
   c. The **foolish** child had no packed lunch.

Key words
antonym

Vocabulary 33

---

100 English Lessons Year 6 links:

- Starter activity 17 (page 14): Synonyms and antonyms
- Autumn 1, Week 5 (page 33): Lesson 5, There and back again
- Summer 2, Week 4 (pages 188–190): write about street children
- Summer 2, Week 6 (pages 194–196): compose a poem

Year 6 Practice Book links:

- (pages 48–49): Synonyms and antonyms

Year 6 Vocabulary 115

Informal and formal vocabulary

Prior learning

- Know that language can be changed to suit the audience.

Learn

- Explain the words 'formal' and 'informal' to the children, giving examples of the different spoken and written situations where they may apply.

- Ask for two volunteers to come to the front to act with you in separate role plays. In the first role play, the volunteer will play a parent new to the school and you will be the teacher. In the second role play, the volunteer will play a pupil new to the school and you will be another pupil. In both cases, the newcomer is trying to find out what the school is like.

- Once you have performed the role plays, ask the class about the language used and how it differed.

- Whether a text is to be formal or informal should be considered during writing. *100 English Lessons Year 6* indicates this throughout writing activities. There are also links to active and passive voice (see pages 96–97 of this book) and the subjunctive (see pages 98–99 of this book).

Curriculum objectives

- To understand the difference between structures typical of informal speech and structures appropriate for formal speech and writing. (Grammar appendix)

Success criteria

- I can adapt my use of vocabulary for formal and informal situations.

Informal and formal vocabulary

Learn

What is the difference between informal or formal vocabulary?

We use different vocabulary in different situations and in different kinds of writing. You probably wouldn't talk to your head teacher in the way that you would talk to your baby sister!

Formal vocabulary: is used in official documents or situations.

Informal vocabulary: is used in more personal documents when in relaxed situations.

Formal vocabulary	Informal vocabulary
Talking with people in authority	Talking with friends or family
Giving a speech in school	Asking for things in shops
Interviews	Diaries
News bulletins/weather reports	Notes
Letters of application for jobs	E-mails and texts

Formal vocabulary uses Standard English. It may use words and phrases that are specifically related to the situation, for example, in a courtroom.
Informal vocabulary may use slang. It may use simpler words.

Formal vocabulary	Informal vocabulary
discover	find out
request	ask for
enter	go in
our house	ours

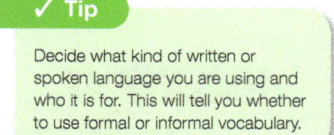

✓ Tip

Decide what kind of written or spoken language you are using and who it is for. This will tell you whether to use formal or informal vocabulary.

Your meaning can be exactly the same using formal or informal vocabulary.

"**I'm sorry sir**, but you are not **permitted** to park your car here. It is a **restricted area**."
— Formal vocabulary —

"**Oi**, you can't park here, **mate**. It's a **no-parking zone**."
— Informal vocabulary —

34 Vocabulary

116 Year 6 Vocabulary

Talk

- Give out some role-play cards for the children to improvise in pairs or threes. Some will be formal, some informal. Ask confident children to show their scenes to the class. Again, talk about the vocabulary that was used.

Activities

- Having considered the answers to activity 1, ask the children to take on a role different to themselves, for instance a pensioner, a police officer or a football player. Ask them to pick one of the situations and write in role using formal or informal language as appropriate.
- Compile a set of improvisation cards: some with roles, some with settings, some with suggestions for dialogue, some with 'formal' or 'informal' written on them. As a whole class or in groups, participants randomly turn over cards to create a situation for improvisation. For instance, it may end up being a postal worker, a doctor, the middle of a field, asking for directions, formal. The situations may end up very bizarre, but the emphasis is on the use of language.

Activities

1. Which of these situations require formal vocabulary and which need informal?
   - A shopping list
   - A reply to a written wedding invitation
   - A presentation to your class
   - A telephone bill
   - A phone call to a friend
   - A postcard to your sister from your holiday

2. Complete this table. You may need to use a dictionary to help you.

Formal vocabulary	Informal vocabulary
commence	
conclude	
renovate	
beverage	

3. Rewrite this telephone conversation using formal vocabulary.

   Sonny: Yow Tezza, Sonny here!
   Tezza: Hi Sonny. Whatcha after?
   Sonny: You done that homework? It's rock hard.
   Tezza: Nah. I'm gonna do it afters. There's a sound proggy on the telly I wanna watch first.
   Sonny: Giz a bell when you do. I'm gonna put me feet up for a bit then have a go at it.

4. With a partner, write a playscript:
   a. in which a young person uses informal vocabulary to explain to his or her parent why they were late for school.
   b. Rewrite the playscript so that the young person uses formal vocabulary to explain the lateness to their head teacher.

5. With a partner, design:
   a. a flyer for a window-cleaning company
   b. headed paper for your school.

   You will need to decide whether to use formal or informal vocabulary.

6. Share your designs with another pair. Explain where and how you have used formal and informal language.

Vocabulary 35

100 English Lessons Year 6 links:

- Autumn 2, Week 1 (pages 51–53): write formal instructions
- Autumn 2, Week 2 (pages 54–56): role-play a trial scene
- Spring 1, Week 2 (page 88): Lesson 5, Formal speech
- Spring 1, Assess and review (pages 102–103): Formal and informal language
- Spring 2, Week 5 (pages 127–129): write a newspaper article
- Summer 2, Week 1 (page 181): Lesson 4, Informal dialogue
- Summer 2, Week 2 (pages 182–184): write a workhouse report

Year 6 Practice Book links:

- (page 50): Formal to informal
- (page 51): Informal to formal
- (page 52): Formal or informal?

Year 6 Vocabulary 117

Letter strings: 'ought' and Letter strings: 'ough'

Prior learning

- Know that 'ough' can make different sounds.

Learn

- Using as many 'ough' and 'ought' strings as possible, write an introduction to the lesson. In advance of delivering your opening speech, tell the children that the introduction contains many words with the same letter string. Can they spot the string?

- An example of your opening could be: 'Though today's work may be tough, I have thought thoroughly about how to plough through it…'
- Once the letter strings have been identified, ask the children if they notice anything about how the words sound. Then talk about the differences in pronunciation.

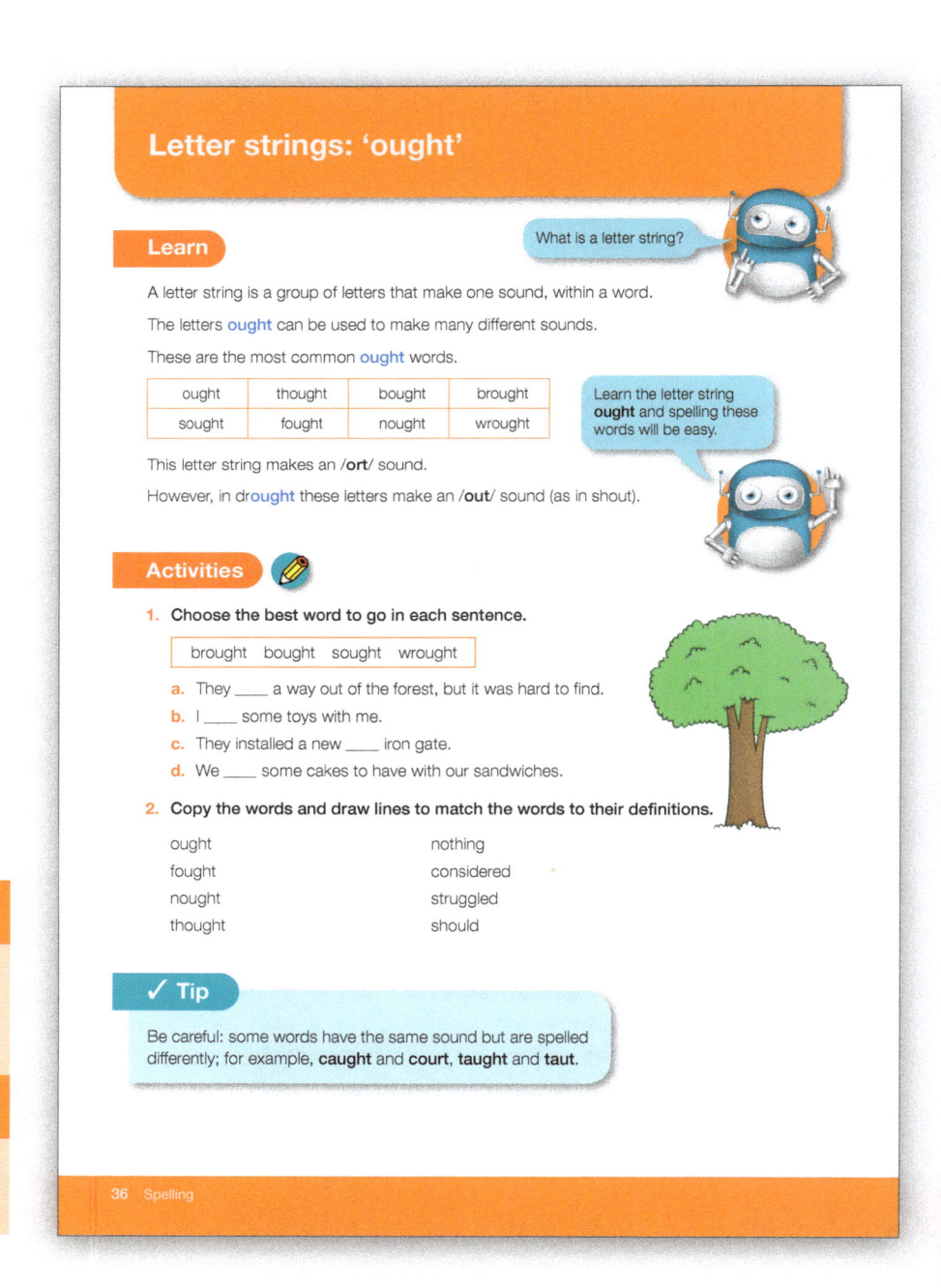

Curriculum objectives

- To spell words containing the letter string 'ough'. (Spelling appendix)

Success criteria

- I can spell words with the letter strings 'ough' and 'ought'.

Letter strings: 'ought'

Learn

What is a letter string?

A letter string is a group of letters that make one sound, within a word.

The letters **ough** can be used to make many different sounds.

These are the most common **ough** words.

ought	thought	bought	brought
sought	fought	nought	wrought

Learn the letter string **ought** and spelling these words will be easy.

This letter string makes an /ort/ sound.

However, in dr**ough**t these letters make an /**out**/ sound (as in shout).

Activities

1. Choose the best word to go in each sentence.

   | brought bought sought wrought |

   a. They ___ a way out of the forest, but it was hard to find.
   b. I ___ some toys with me.
   c. They installed a new ___ iron gate.
   d. We ___ some cakes to have with our sandwiches.

2. Copy the words and draw lines to match the words to their definitions.

   ought   nothing
   fought   considered
   nought   struggled
   thought   should

✓ Tip

Be careful: some words have the same sound but are spelled differently; for example, **caught** and **court**, **taught** and **taut**.

Write

- Give the children a sheet with lists of 'ough' and 'ought' words. Ask them to improvise conversations in pairs or threes where, each time they speak, they use one of the words. The dialogue can be realistic or fantastic. The challenge is to use one of the words each time. Two would be great. Three would be amazing!

- For example:
  - A: I thought this was a tough lesson.
  - B: I have a cough today. I don't know whether I will get through it.
  - C: I feel rough.
  - A: I bought a plough last night and made some dough.
  - B: I thought you were acting oddly!

Activities

- Once all of the textbook activities are complete, ask the children to write a follow-up paragraph using the target spellings. It could be the opening of a story, a factual account or a piece of nonsense writing, perhaps a poem.
- Make some display posters containing groups of 'ough' and 'ought' words which make the same sounds.
- Class chanting could be used to reinforce the different sounds of the spellings.

Letter strings: 'ough'

Learn

What sound does the letter string **ough** make?

The letter string ough makes several sounds: /uff/ (as in stuff); /off/; /oo/ (as in moon); /oe/ (as in toe); and /ow/ (as in cow).

Using the letter string ough can be tricky because it can make so many sounds. Here are some examples of each sound.

'uff' (as in cuff)	'off'	'oo' (as in moon)	'oe' (as in toe)	'ow' (as in cow)
rough	cough	through	though	bough
tough	trough		dough	plough

Some ough words don't belong in these groups:

| thorough | borough |

These words both have an /uh/ sound at the end.

✓ Tip

Say the word, then work out which sound it makes.

Activities

1. Use these 'ough' words to make new words to fit in each space.

   | dough | rough | tough |

   a. They ___ worked out how to make the model.
   b. The doors were made of ___ glass.
   c. We bought some ___ to eat at the fairground.

2. Write the 'ough' words to match each definition.

Definition	Word
area	
branch	
cultivate	
sufficient	
animal food container	

Spelling 37

100 English Lessons Year 6 links:

- Spring 2, Week 2 (page 120): Lesson 5, Back cover blurbs
- Spring 2, Assess and review (page 133): Commonly misspelled words
- Summer 2, Week 2 (page 183): Lesson 3, The workhouse overseer

Year 6 Practice Book links:

- (pages 24–27): Rough stuff!

Year 6 Spelling 119

Silent letters

Prior learning

- Know that silent letters exist in a range of words, already using simpler ones.

Learn

- In a mysterious way, tell the children that silence is golden and you are challenging them to find the gold. Begin to enigmatically say short sentences with silent letters in them. Be as weird as you like and keep repeating the phrase 'Silence is golden: find the gold.' Ideas for weird sentences could include:
  - I have the knowledge of the knights.
  - The thistle is with the whistle in the castle.
  - Autumn is solemn.

Curriculum objectives

- To spell some words with 'silent' letters.

Success criteria

- I can spell some words with 'silent' letters.

100 English Lessons Year 6 links:

- Starter activity 15 (page 14): Silent letters
- Summer 2, Week 2 (page 182–184): Lesson 2 and Lesson 5
- Summer 2, Week 3 (page 187): Lesson 5, Polish the article
- Summer 2, Assess and review (page 197): Silent letters

Year 6 Practice Book links:

- (pages 28–29): Silent knight

- Once someone is on the right track, such as, 'Is it to do with what you're saying?', reply with something like, 'Yes, there is silence in what I am saying. Find the gold!'
- If you have a wizard's hat to hand, wear it. If someone has clearly worked it out, invite them to come to the front to wear the hat as your apprentice, delivering some more clues.

Activities

- In groups, ask the children to focus one at a time on each of the target spellings. They are to say it as it is written – for instance, 'sub-tle' – perhaps using a funny voice or action. Challenge them to make up their own mnemonics such as 'a sub-title has subtle endings'.

Write

- Challenge the children to write a poem entitled 'The Silent Knight' using as many of the new spellings as possible.

Silent letters

Learn

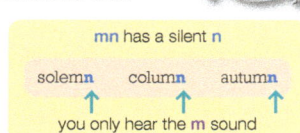

When are silent letters used?

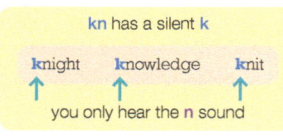

Silent letters are used to write a sound – but you can't hear them when you say the word.

There are lots of silent letters. They often pair up with another letter.

bt has a silent b
dou**b**t   de**b**t   su**b**tle
you only hear the t sound

mn has a silent n
sole**mn**   colum**n**   autum**n**
you only hear the m sound

s can be a silent s
i**s**land   ai**s**le   debri**s**
you cannot hear the s sound

kn has a silent k
knight   **k**nowledge   **k**nit
you only hear the n sound

st has a silent t
thi**st**le   whi**st**le   ca**st**le
you only hear the s sound

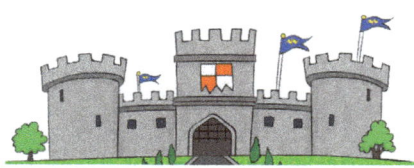

Activities

1. Underline the silent letter in each word in bold.
   a. They went over the bridge to the **Isle** of Anglesey.
   b. Look at the third **column**.
   c. We are **indebted** to you, thanks to all your efforts.
   d. Caitlin saw a **mistle** thrush in the garden.

2. Write the correct spelling for each word.
   a. dought/doubt/dout
   b. isle/iall/iel
   c. condam/condemn/condem
   d. brissle/brissel/bristle

✓ Tip

To help you spell a word, pronounce it with the silent letter: **sub–tle**. If you can hear each letter, you will use it when writing the word.

'c' or 's'?

Prior learning

- Know that the /s/ sound can also be spelled with a 'c'.

Learn

- Invent some tongue-twisters that contain a mixture of words beginning with 'c' and 's'. Say them out loud to the class. For instance:
  - Sausages certainly smell spectacular.
  - I saw some seriously solid cement on Sunday.
- Ask the children if they can spot what is going on. If they say that you're using tongue-twisters or repeating the /s/ sound, encourage them to be more specific.
- Once it has been established that you are using both 'c' and 's' words, write them on the whiteboard.
- Review the rules in the textbook together.

Activities

- Complete the activities in the textbook.
- The activity in the *Practice Book* and *100 English Lessons Year 6* focus on 'c' and 's' in homophones such as 'advice' and 'advise' which you may like to extend the teaching to include.
- Ask the children to invent sentences that contain at least one 'c' and one 's' word. For example, 'I saw seven cygnets on the river'.

Write

- Set the challenge of composing a description of the sea that contains as many different /s/ sounds as possible, both with 'c' and 's' spellings.

Curriculum objectives

- To use knowledge of morphology and etymology in spelling and understand that the spelling of some words needs to be learned specifically, as listed in the Spelling appendix.

Success criteria

- I can spell a range of words beginning with or containing 'c' or 's'.

100 English Lessons Year 6 links:

- Autumn 2, Week 3 (page 58): Lesson 2, Tricky homophones

Year 6 Practice Book links:

- (pages 30–32): Advice or advise?

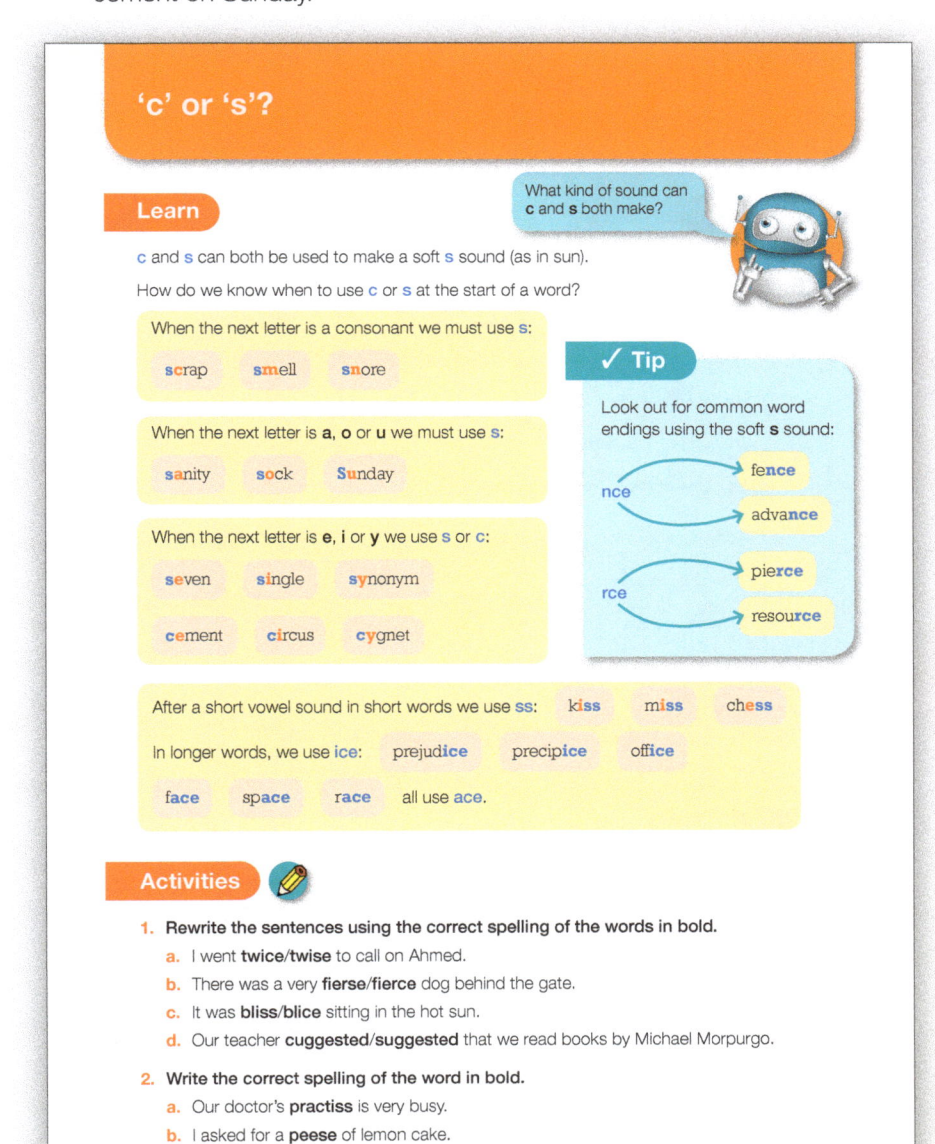

'c' or 's'?

Learn

What kind of sound can c and s both make?

c and s can both be used to make a soft s sound (as in sun).

How do we know when to use c or s at the start of a word?

When the next letter is a consonant we must use s:

scrap **s**mell **s**nore

When the next letter is **a**, **o** or **u** we must use s:

sanity **s**ock **S**unday

When the next letter is **e**, **i** or **y** we use s or c:

seven **s**ingle **s**ynonym

cement **c**ircus **c**ygnet

✓ Tip

Look out for common word endings using the soft **s** sound:

nce → fe**nce**
nce → adva**nce**

rce → pie**rce**
rce → resou**rce**

After a short vowel sound in short words we use ss: ki**ss** mi**ss** che**ss**

In longer words, we use ice: preju**dice** precip**ice** off**ice**

f**ace** sp**ace** r**ace** all use **ace**.

Activities

1. Rewrite the sentences using the correct spelling of the words in bold.
   a. I went **twice/twise** to call on Ahmed.
   b. There was a very **fierse/fierce** dog behind the gate.
   c. It was **bliss/blice** sitting in the hot sun.
   d. Our teacher **cuggested/suggested** that we read books by Michael Morpurgo.

2. Write the correct spelling of the word in bold.
   a. Our doctor's **practiss** is very busy.
   b. I asked for a **peese** of lemon cake.

Year 6 Spelling 121

Adding 'cious' or 'tious'

Prior learning

- Know that the /sh/ sound can be spelled in different ways.

Learn

- Begin the lesson by saying 'Shh' until the class is quiet. Write it on the whiteboard if necessary. Accompany it with some weird actions. Don't say another word if possible from the moment the children enter. If needed, only say words with the /sh/ sound in them, in an enigmatic way.

- Once you have everyone's attention, start saying 'cious' and 'tious' words aloud, perhaps linking them to the children in a fun way. For instance, if someone comes in late, say, 'Atrocious!' in a silly, non-aggressive manner; or pick up a novel from a desk and say, 'Fictitious!'

- Focus on the spellings of these words, use the textbook to support this.

Activities

- Use the activities in the textbook and on pages 6–7 of the *Year 6 Practice Book* to consolidate understanding.
- Use the 'I owe you' (IOU) mnemonic to run a fun test:
  - Teacher: What do you owe me to spell fictitious? A 't' or a 'c'?
  - Pupil: I owe you a 't'! T-I-O-U-S. Yes?
  - Teacher: Yes!

Curriculum objectives

- To spell endings which sound like /shus/ spelled 'cious' or 'tious'. (Spelling appendix)

Success criteria

- I can spell a range of words ending 'cious' or 'tious'.

100 English Lessons Year 6 links:

- Starter activity 3 (page 11): Word endings
- Autumn 1, Week 2 (page 22): Lesson 1, Brazil leaflet – researching

Year 6 Practice Book links:

- (pages 6–7): Very suspicious…

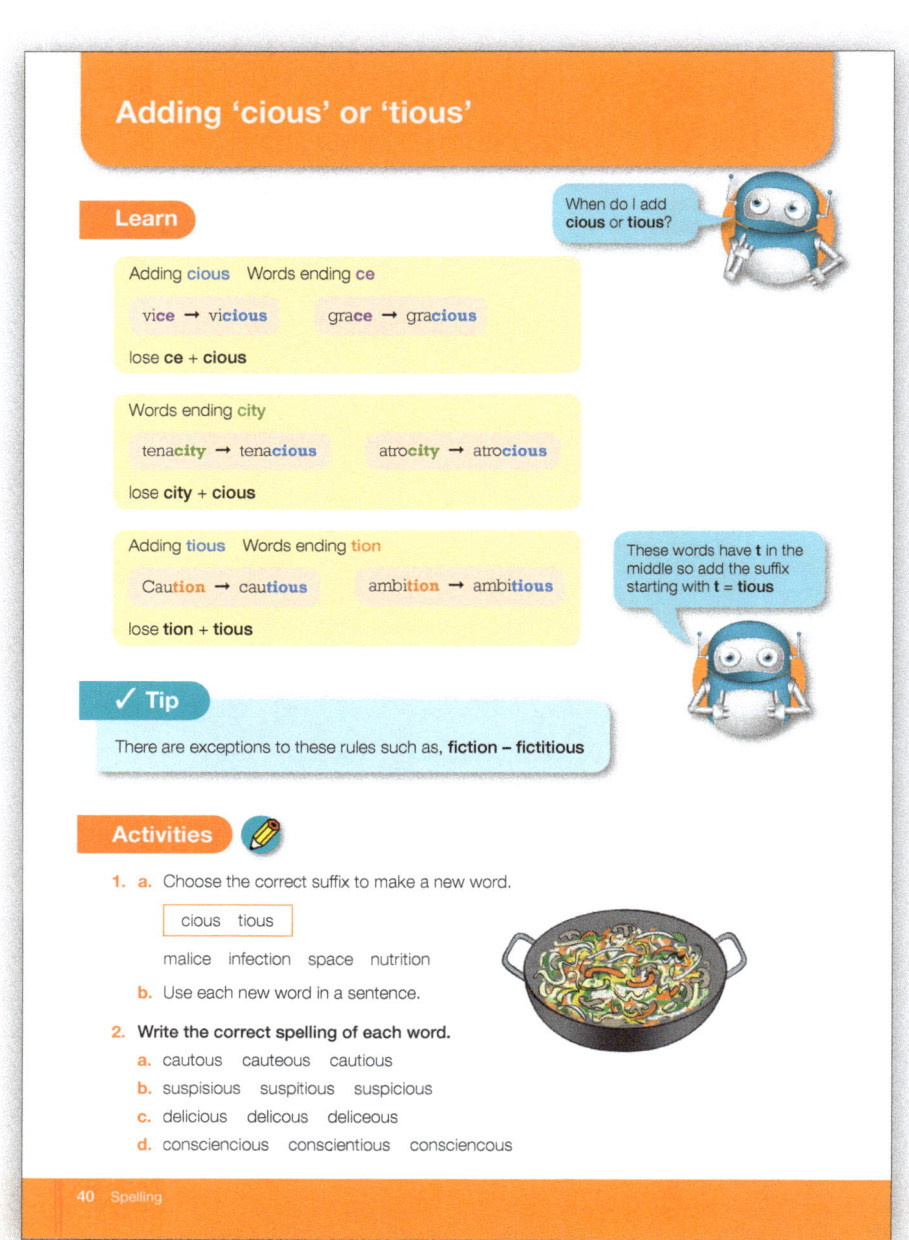

Adding 'cious' or 'tious'

Learn

When do I add **cious** or **tious**?

Adding cious Words ending **ce**

vi**ce** → vi**cious**   gra**ce** → gra**cious**

lose **ce** + **cious**

Words ending **city**

tena**city** → tena**cious**   atro**city** → atro**cious**

lose **city** + **cious**

Adding tious Words ending **tion**

Cau**tion** → cau**tious**   ambi**tion** → ambi**tious**

lose **tion** + **tious**

These words have **t** in the middle so add the suffix starting with **t = tious**

✓ Tip

There are exceptions to these rules such as, **fiction – fictitious**

Activities

1. a. Choose the correct suffix to make a new word.

   | cious tious |

   malice   infection   space   nutrition

   b. Use each new word in a sentence.

2. Write the correct spelling of each word.
   a. cautous   cauteous   cautious
   b. suspisious   suspitious   suspicious
   c. delicious   delicous   deliceous
   d. consciencious   conscientious   consciencous

40 Spelling

---

122 Year 6 Spelling

Adding 'tial' or 'cial'

Prior learning

- Know that the /sh/ sound can be spelled in different ways.

Learn

- If delivering this lesson directly after the 'tious'/'cious' lesson, a repetition of the previous starter will have a comic effect. The children will be halfway to guessing what you are up to this time, but they will realise it's not quite the same.

- Review the teaching in the textbook together and make sure children understand and can recall the words. Try to think of more examples – do they fit the rule or are they exceptions?

Activities

- Use the activities in the textbook and on pages 8–9 of the *Year 6 Practice Book* to consolidate understanding.
- Make some wall charts to collect 'tial' and 'cial' words.

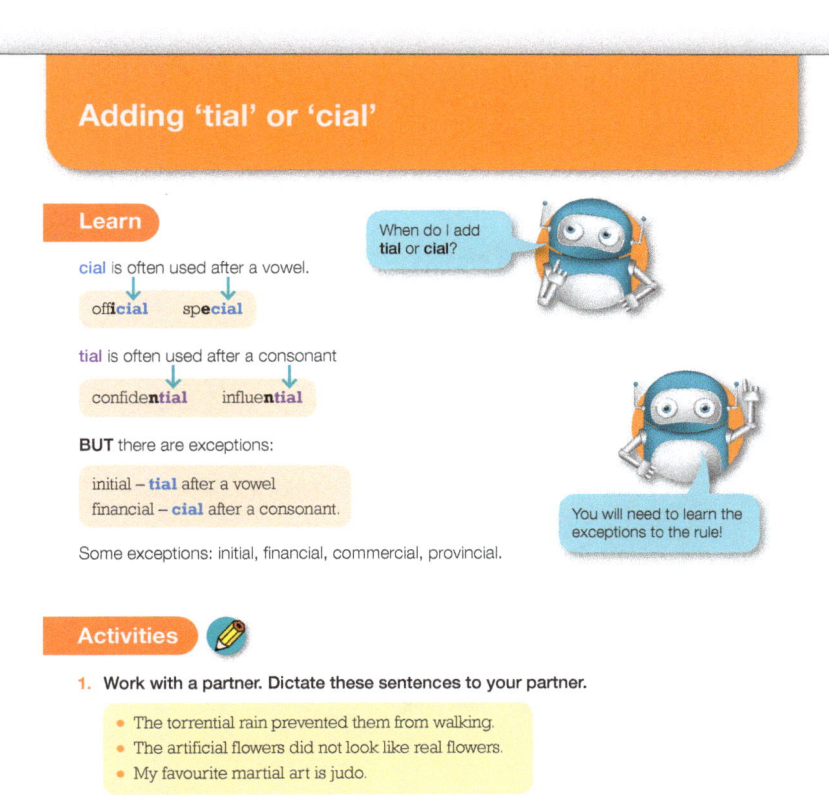

Adding 'tial' or 'cial'

Learn

cial is often used after a vowel.

offi**cial**   spe**cial**

tial is often used after a consonant

confide**ntial**   influe**ntial**

BUT there are exceptions:

initial – **tial** after a vowel
financial – **cial** after a consonant.

Some exceptions: initial, financial, commercial, provincial.

When do I add **tial** *or* **cial***?*

You will need to learn the exceptions to the rule!

Activities

1. Work with a partner. Dictate these sentences to your partner.
   - The torrential rain prevented them from walking.
   - The artificial flowers did not look like real flowers.
   - My favourite martial art is judo.

   Now highlight any spelling mistakes. Can your partner work out how they should have been spelled?

2. Work with a partner. Ask your partner to dictate these sentences to you.
   - The official accident report was released yesterday.
   - The social club has a disco on Saturday.
   - Katie has the potential to be an excellent swimmer.

   Now highlight any spelling mistakes. Can you work out how they should have been spelled?

3. Look at the 'tial' and 'cial' words in the above sentences. Write the words into columns under the headings: 'tial' or 'cial'.

Spelling 41

Curriculum objectives

- To spell endings which sound like /shul/. (Spelling appendix)

Success criteria

- I can spell some words that end with 'tial' or 'cial'.

100 English Lessons Year 6 links:

- Starter activity 3 (page 11): Word endings
- Autumn 1, Assess and review (page 37): Words ending in /shul/; using a dictionary to check spelling

Year 6 Practice Book links:

- (pages 8–9): Crucial words

Adding 'able' or 'ably' and Adding 'ible' or 'ibly'

Prior learning
- Know the more common 'able' and 'ible' spellings.

Learn
- Explain to the children that the 'able'/'ible' spellings are quite difficult to learn and that it will take time and repetition to get them correct.
- Use the lessons in *100 English Lessons Year 6* to support the learning.

Talk
- Ask the children to create some fun dialogue where the characters use 'able'/'ible'/'ably'/'ibly' words but pronounce the vowel sounds in a very exaggerated way. Ask confident volunteers to perform their dialogues for the class.

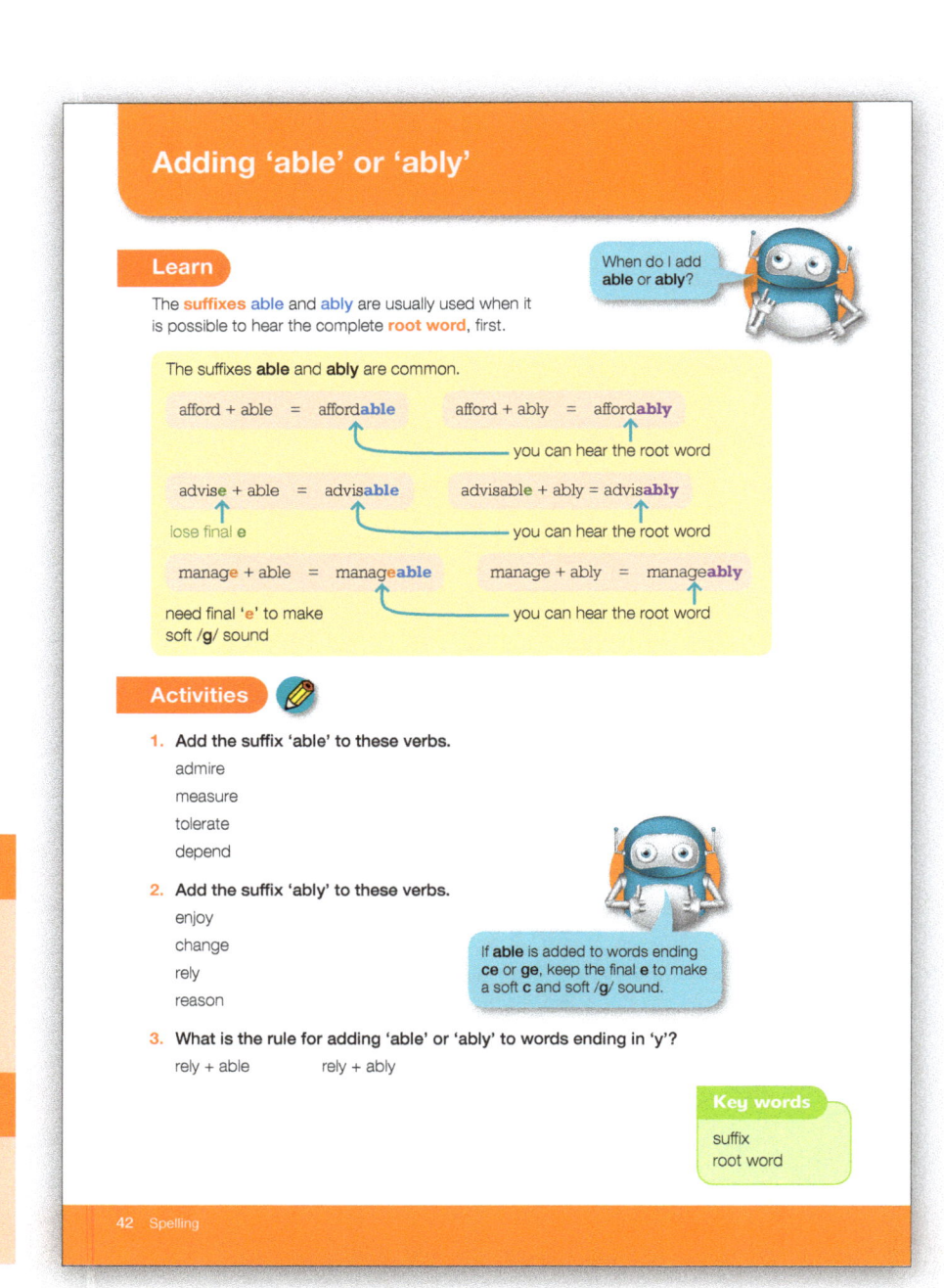

Curriculum objectives
- To spell words ending in 'able' and 'ible'. (Spelling appendix)
- To spell words ending in 'ably' and 'ibly'. (Spelling appendix)

Success criteria
- I can spell a range of words ending with 'able, 'ible', 'ably' and 'ibly'.

Adding 'able' or 'ably'

Learn

When do I add **able** or **ably**?

The **suffixes** **able** and **ably** are usually used when it is possible to hear the complete **root word**, first.

The suffixes **able** and **ably** are common.

afford + able = afford**able**   afford + ably = afford**ably**
                                    ↑
                          you can hear the root word

advise + able = advis**able**   advisable + ably = advis**ably**
↑   ↑
lose final e   you can hear the root word

manag**e** + able = manage**able**   manage + ably = manage**ably**
                                    ↑
need final 'e' to make   you can hear the root word
soft /g/ sound

Activities

1. Add the suffix 'able' to these verbs.
   admire
   measure
   tolerate
   depend

2. Add the suffix 'ably' to these verbs.
   enjoy
   change
   rely
   reason

   If **able** is added to words ending **ce** or **ge**, keep the final **e** to make a soft **c** and soft /g/ sound.

3. What is the rule for adding 'able' or 'ably' to words ending in 'y'?
   rely + able   rely + ably

Key words
suffix
root word

Activities

- Use the activities in the textbook and on pages 14–17 of the *Year 6 Practice Book* to consolidate understanding.
- Ask the children to create mnemonics to remember certain spellings. For example, 'An affordable table' or 'a sensible bible'. Tell them that creating a picture of an action in your head can help you to recall correct spellings

Write

- Ask the children to write the words in context, either in separate sentences or as part of a story. Underline the target spellings to draw attention to them.
- Challenge the children to create two verses of a poem. The first verse should contain 'able' and 'ably' words; the second verse should contain 'ible' and 'ibly' words.

Adding 'ible' or 'ibly'

When do I add ibly or ably?

Learn

The suffixes **ible** and **ibly** are usually used when you cannot hear the complete root word.

The **ible** and **ibly** suffixes are not as common.

neg**lect** + ible   =   **neg**l**ible**
↑   ↑
lose final syllable   you hear only part of the root word

comprehen**d** + ibly   =   comprehen**sibly**
↑   ↑
change final letter   you hear only part of the root word

Not all words obey the rule!

forc**e** + ible   =   forcible
↑   ↑
lose final e   you can hear the root word

Activities

1. Copy and complete the root words, adding the suffixes 'ible' and 'ibly'.

Root word	+ ible	+ ibly
leger		
sense		
reverse		
defend		

You may need to change part of the root word.

2. Rewrite each sentence, filling in the missing word ending with 'ible'.
   a. The burnt pie was totally ____.
   b. His writing was ____.

3. Rewrite each sentence, filling in the missing word ending with 'ibly'.
   a. The burglars had ____ entered the property.
   b. The child was ____ upset after the fall.

Spelling 43

---

100 English Lessons Year 6 links:

- Starter activity 3 (page 11): Word endings
- Autumn 1, Week 4 (page 29): Lesson 2, Plotting the journey
- Summer 1, Assess and review (pages 165): Words ending in '-ible' and '-able'

Year 6 Practice Book links:

- (pages 14–17): Possibly confusable?

'ei' after 'c'

Prior learning

- Know the 'i' before 'e' except after 'c', when the sound is /ee/ mnemonic.

Learn

- Write the target spellings on the whiteboard. In a separate column, write up words which are spelled 'ei' without a 'c'. Point out the difference in sound from /ee/ to /ay/.
- Write some odd ones such as 'seize', 'siege' and 'weird' for separate discussion – where do they fit in? Do they follow the rule or are they exceptions?
- Stress that English spelling can sometimes be frustrating. There are rules to help, but there are also words which don't follow the rules and just have to be learned in a different way.

Activities

- Use the activities in the textbook and on pages 22–23 of the *Year 6 Practice Book* to consolidate understanding.
- Extend the practice by writing story openings or poems which contain the target spellings.
- Use the 'look, cover, write, check' method to practise them further.

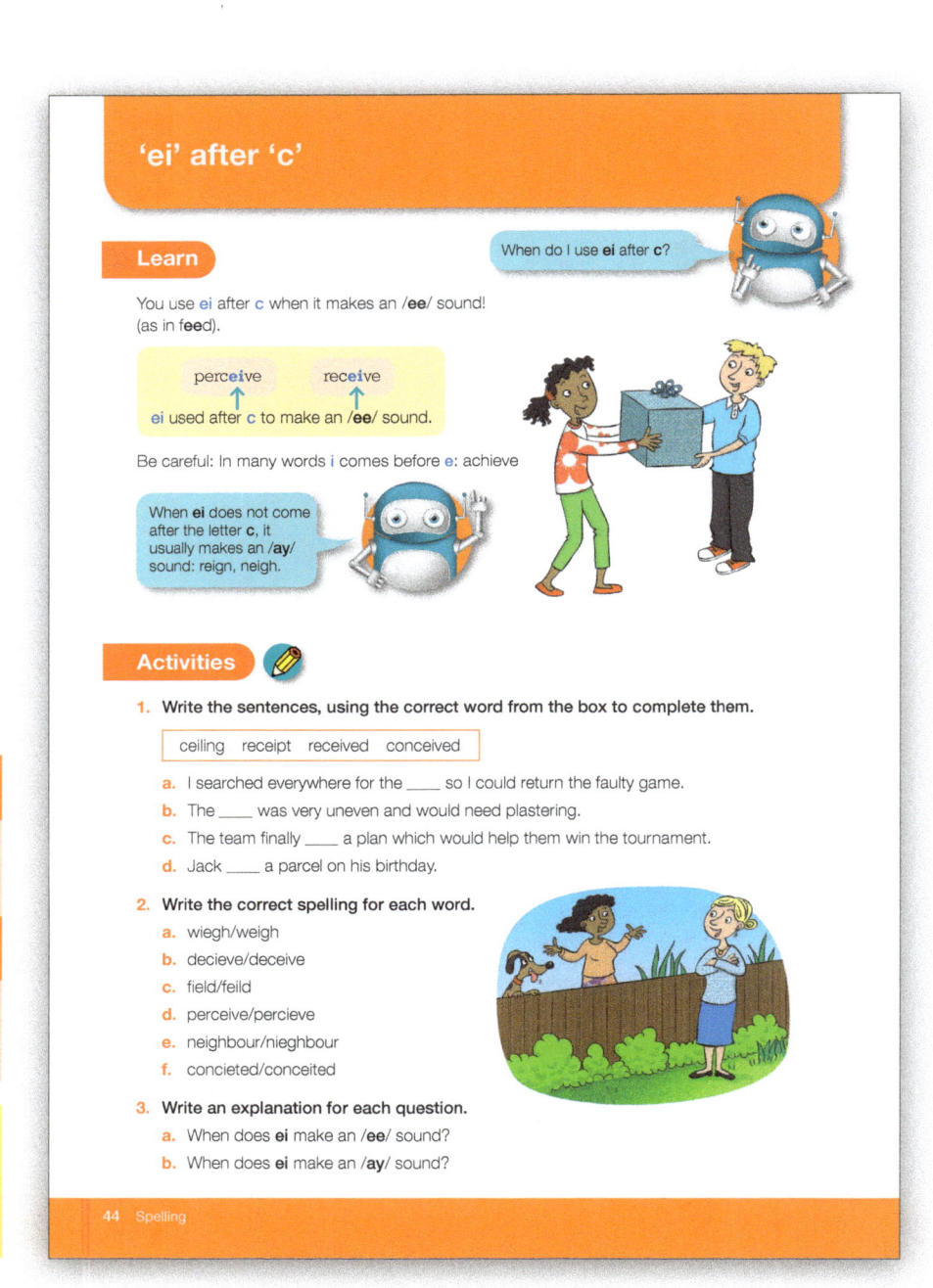

Curriculum objectives

- To spell words with the /ee/ sound spelled 'ei' after 'c'.

Success criteria

- I can spell words with 'ei' after 'c'.

Year 6 Practice Book links:

- (pages 22–23): Is it 'ie' or 'ei'?

'ei' after 'c'

Learn

When do I use **ei** after **c**?

You use **ei** after **c** when it makes an /**ee**/ sound! (as in f**ee**d).

perc**ei**ve   rec**ei**ve

ei used after **c** to make an /**ee**/ sound.

Be careful: In many words **i** comes before **e**: ach**ie**ve

When **ei** does not come after the letter **c**, it usually makes an /**ay**/ sound: r**ei**gn, n**ei**gh.

Activities

1. Write the sentences, using the correct word from the box to complete them.

   ceiling   receipt   received   conceived

   a. I searched everywhere for the ____ so I could return the faulty game.
   b. The ____ was very uneven and would need plastering.
   c. The team finally ____ a plan which would help them win the tournament.
   d. Jack ____ a parcel on his birthday.

2. Write the correct spelling for each word.
   a. wiegh/weigh
   b. decieve/deceive
   c. field/feild
   d. perceive/percieve
   e. neighbour/nieghbour
   f. concieted/conceited

3. Write an explanation for each question.
   a. When does **ei** make an /**ee**/ sound?
   b. When does **ei** make an /**ay**/ sound?

Tricky words

Prior learning

- Know that some words are difficult to learn and will take time.
- Know that root words can help to work out longer spellings.

Learn

- Write the target spellings on the board. Ask pairs to use the 'look, cover, write, check' method to have a go at learning some of the words from the list. You may wish to use words from the Years 5–6 word list from the spelling appendix in the National Curriculum.
- Explain that a knowledge of root words can help; for instance knowing that 'explanation' comes from the root word 'explain', will make the longer word easier to spell.

Talk

- Ask pairs to say the target words out loud to each other, stressing each syllable, even if it makes the word sound odd.

Activities

- Use the activities in the textbook to consolidate understanding.
- Ask the children to include the target spellings in standalone sentences, as part of a story opener or in a poem.

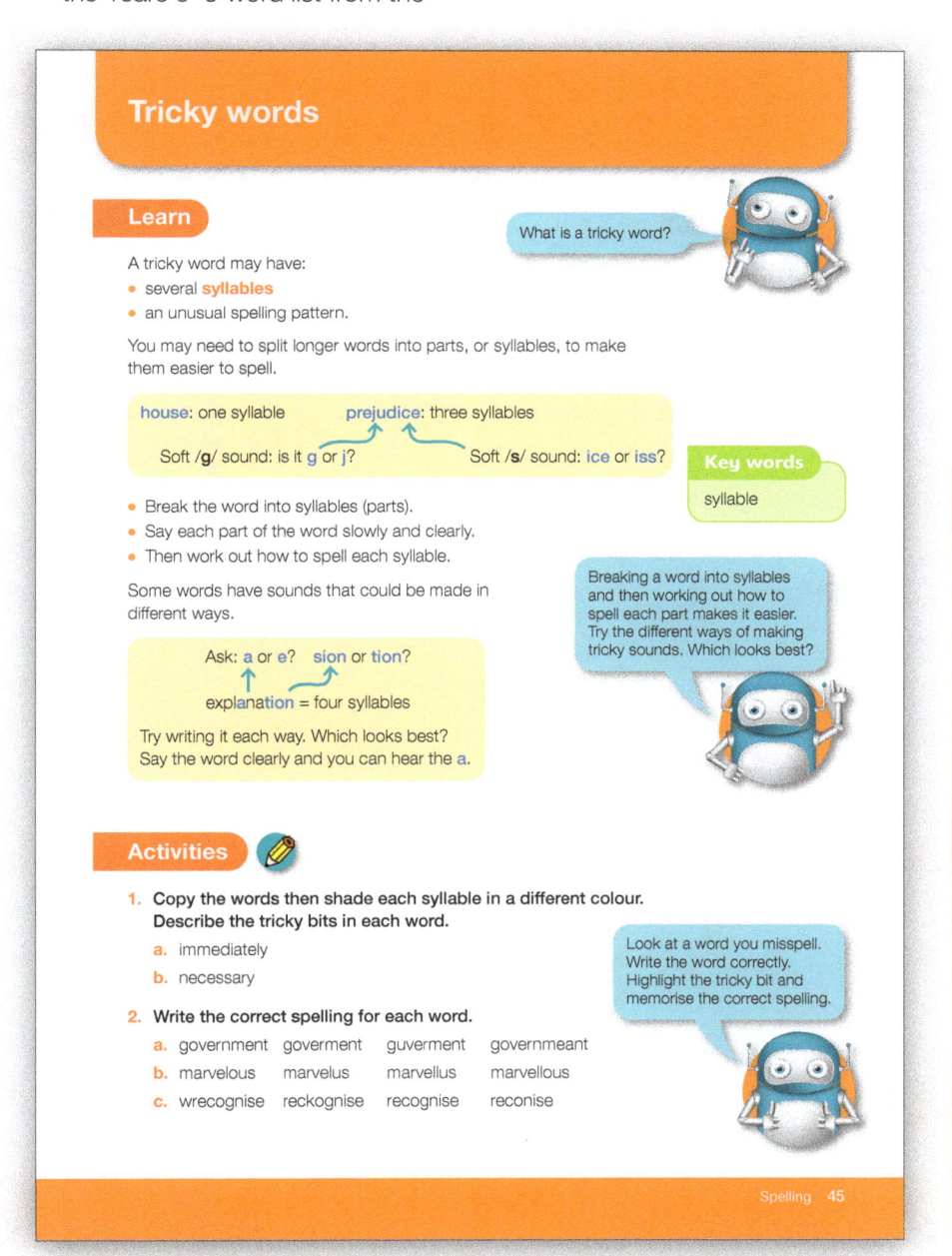

Tricky words

Learn

What is a tricky word?

A tricky word may have:
- several **syllables**
- an unusual spelling pattern.

You may need to split longer words into parts, or syllables, to make them easier to spell.

house: one syllable   prejudice: three syllables
Soft /g/ sound: is it g or j?   Soft /s/ sound: ice or iss?

Key words
syllable

- Break the word into syllables (parts).
- Say each part of the word slowly and clearly.
- Then work out how to spell each syllable.

Some words have sounds that could be made in different ways.

Ask: a or e?   sion or tion?
explanation = four syllables

Breaking a word into syllables and then working out how to spell each part makes it easier. Try the different ways of making tricky sounds. Which looks best?

Try writing it each way. Which looks best? Say the word clearly and you can hear the a.

Activities

1. Copy the words then shade each syllable in a different colour. Describe the tricky bits in each word.
   a. immediately
   b. necessary

2. Write the correct spelling for each word.
   a. government   goverment   guverment   governmeant
   b. marvelous   marvulus   marvellus   marvellous
   c. wrecognise   reckognise recognise   reconise

Look at a word you misspell. Write the word correctly. Highlight the tricky bit and memorise the correct spelling.

Spelling 45

Curriculum objectives

- To use knowledge of morphology and etymology in spelling and understand that the spelling of some words needs to be learned specifically, as listed in the Spelling appendix.

Success criteria

- I can use syllables, sounding out and a knowledge of root words to help with tricky words.

100 English Lessons Year 6 links:

- Spring 1, Assess and review (page 101): Archaic vocabulary

Year 6 Spelling 127

Homophones

Prior learning

- Know that some words sound the same but are spelled differently.

Learn

- Make up some sentences containing the target spellings and read them aloud to the class, asking if anyone knows what the two homophones mean and how to spell them.
- Here are some examples:
  - The false prophet was only in it for financial profit.
  - The principal of the college had only one principle – to learn.
- This morning I was mourning the loss of my pet.
- The stationary van was full of stationery.

Curriculum objectives

- To continue to distinguish between homophones and other words which are often confused.

Success criteria

- I know the different spellings of a range of homophones.

Homophones

Learn

What is a homophone?

A **homophone** is a pair of words that sound the same but are spelled differently.

There are lots of homophones. Here are a few examples.

| principal | → the leader |
| principle | → a belief |

| prophet | → someone who foretells the future |
| profit | → a financial gain |

I awoke early this **morning**. → the start of the day

They are in **mourning** following the king's death. → in sorrow (following a death)

license → (verb) to allow
They were **licensed** to fish on this part of the river.

licence → (noun) a permit which allows you to do something
My television **licence** has expired.

stationary → not moving
The car was **stationary**. (Think: There is **ar** in **c**ar and station**ar**y!)

stationery → office paper/envelopes and materials
I ordered some more **stationery** for the office.
(Think: stationery includes paper. There is **er** in pap**er** and station**er**y!)

✓ **Tip**

Can you find an easy way to remember what a pair of homophones mean? For example: **here** or **hear**. Hear has **ear** hiding in it!

Talk

- Use starter activity 4 from *100 English Lessons Year 6*. Having played the game, leave the words up on the board and invite pairs to the front to hold an improvised conversation using words selected at random. Invite the audience members to shout 'Freeze!' at any point when they hear one of the words being used – can they now pick the right spelling from the board?

Activities

- Challenge the children to write sentences that contain two homophones. Make it harder by asking them to build the sentences into the opening of a story or a description.
- Ask the children to design posters to go around the school corridors to help younger children understand the different spellings of homophones.
- Having completed the word search or crossword on pages 45 and 46 of the *Practice Book*, give the children some squared paper and ask them to create one of their own using different homophones. They then give it to a neighbour to solve.
- Ask children to use pairs of homophones and to write them in context in sentences or as part of a story.

Activities

1. Copy the sentences and underline the correct homophone for each sentence.
   a. We **heard** / **herd** the firework display in the park.
   b. I wondered **whose** / **who's** car was parked outside my house.
   c. The burglar tried to **steel** / **steal** the television, but it was very heavy.
   d. The porridge was **two** / **to** / **too** hot!

2. Write a sentence for each homophone.
   a. passed   past
   b. guessed   guest

3. Explain the meaning of each homophone.
   a. aloud   allowed
   b. farther father
   c. waste   waist

4. Write the other homophone for these words.
   a. great
   b. dissent
   c. cereal
   d. bridal

Key words
homophone

100 English Lessons Year 6 links:

- Starter activity 4 (page 11): Homophone swat
- Autumn 2, Week 3 (pages 57–59): use homophones to create puns
- Autumn 2, Assess and review (page 69): Homophones and other commonly confused words

Year 6 Practice Book links:

- (pages 33–35): Tricky homophones
- (pages 36–38): Homophone pairs
- (pages 39–41): Spot the difference
- (pages 42–44): Linked pairs
- (page 45): Confused words across and down

Using dictionaries

Prior learning

- Know that dictionaries can be used to find spellings and meanings.

Learn

- Tell the children that regular dictionary usage is one the keys to good learning and that practice makes perfect – the more you use a dictionary, the faster you will get at it and the more useful you will find it.
- Recap how to look for words in a dictionary and how you may need to look for different letters of a word. Use the textbook to support this.
- Play dictionary games. Give the children copies of a dictionary and call out words that they have to locate. Increase the difficulty by asking them to give different information, such as the page number the word is on, the word class or the meaning.
- Encourage the use of dictionary throughout classroom activities.

Curriculum objectives

- To use dictionaries to check the spelling and meaning of words.
- To use the first three or four letters of a word to check spelling, meaning or both of these in a dictionary.

Success criteria

- I can use dictionaries more confidently.

Using dictionaries

Learn

How do I use a dictionary?

Dictionaries are great tools but you need to know how to use them.

Checking spelling
You might not know how to spell some words but will often know how they start. Use the first three or four letters of a word to check spelling.

The key to finding your way around a dictionary quickly is to know the alphabet.

Dictionaries are organised in alphabetical order, with words starting with **a** at the beginning and words starting with **z** at the end. After that, they are arranged by the order of their second letter. Words that start with the same second letter are then arranged in the alphabetical order of their third letters, and so on. It sounds complicated so here is an example from one section of a dictionary. In this example, all of the words begin with **p**.

p**a**rliament, p**e**rsuade, p**h**ysical
ordered by second letter

prej**u**dice, priv**i**lege
ordered by third letter

profe**s**sion, progr**a**mme
ordered by fourth letter

To start using a dictionary, you just need to know what letter the word you want starts with. The more letters you know at the start of the word, the easier it is.

Checking meaning
Sometimes you need to check the meaning of some words to make sure you are using the right ones.

Except and **accept** sound and look very similar. A dictionary will help you to tell the difference.

Except: preposition – meaning a person or thing that is not included in a statement which has just been made. For example, *Our car was easy to find because every car in the car park was blue except ours.*

Accept: verb – meaning to take something that is offered. For example, *I decided to accept my dad's offer of a lift to school.*

Dictionaries also tell you word types.
If you look up *hand*, the dictionary will tell you it could be a *verb*, as in 'to hand something to someone', or it could be a *noun*, as in 'the part of your body at the end of your arm'. This is useful when you use a thesaurus as it helps you choose the correct word to fit the meaning.

Activities

- As an extension to activity 1 in the textbook, ask pairs of children to set each other lists of words to put into alphabetical order. Encourage them to make it difficult by thinking of some words that have the first two or three letters the same.

- Similarly, with activity 5, ask the children to pair up and set each other a challenge.

- As an extension to activity 8, ask the children to use other meanings of the word 'hand' correctly in context.

- Encourage them to use the 'look, cover, write, check' method for practising spellings.

Write

- On an ongoing basis, regularly set aside time for the checking and reviewing of writing just completed. Ask children to use a dictionary to first check their own work and then also check the work of a neighbour. When checking a neighbour, tell them to find and show words in the dictionary, not just tell without showing.

Activities

1. Rewrite these words in the order you would find them in a dictionary.

   | definite | government | achieve | rhyme | bargain | category |
   | language | frequently | embarrass | necessary |

2. Rewrite these words in the order you would find them in a dictionary. Use the first two letters of the words to help you.

   | amateur | mischievous | committee | rhythm | recommend | marvellous |
   | determined | correspond | cemetery | dictionary | restaurant | accommodate |

3. Rewrite these words in the order you would find them in a dictionary. Use the first three or four letters of the words to help you.

   | needle | need | newer | necessary | neither | net |
   | nest | neat | neon | nettle | never | network |

4. Find a word in the dictionary that starts with 'dis' and means *to take someone's attention away from what they are doing*.

5. Rewrite the following words with either a 'c' or an 's' at the beginning. Then look them up in a dictionary to see if you were right.

   | ircle | ervice | ircus | urvive | ease | iren |

6. Use a dictionary to check which of these words have the correct spelling.

   | farewell | mischievous | neccessary | neice | neither | piece | tomorrow |

7. Use a dictionary to help you choose the correct word in these sentences.
   a. I will be going away next **week/weak**.
      I will have to sit down as I am feeling **week/weak**.
   b. I have to sit down as I am feeling **feint/faint**.
      He made a **feint/faint** move that sent me in the wrong direction.
   c. That is not **allowed/aloud**.
      Don't speak **allowed/aloud**.

8. Look up 'hand' in a dictionary. How many different meanings can you find? Use one of the meanings correctly in a sentence.

100 English Lessons Year 6 links:

- Starter activity 7 (page 12): Dictionary and thesaurus game
- Autumn 1, Assess and review (page 37): Words ending in /shul/; using a dictionary to check spelling
- Autumn 2, Week 4 (page 60): Lesson 1, The nonsense world of Lewis Carroll
- Spring 1, Assess and review (page 101): Archaic vocabulary
- Spring 2, Week 1 (page 117): Lesson 4, Proofread and polish
- Spring 2, Week 5 (pages 127–129): read and discuss 'Why You'll Love This Book'

Using a thesaurus

Prior learning

- Be confident with dictionaries and other reference books.

Learn

- You may wish to link this to the teaching of synonyms and antonyms (see pages 114–115 of this book).
- Explain that the thesaurus is an excellent reference book for improving the quality of all writing. It helps us to avoid repetition, to find more accurate words for the impression we are trying to create and helps us bring vaguely familiar or new words into our vocabulary.
- Also give a word of warning – the thesaurus does not provide definitions, so in order to ensure that it is the kind of word we are after, we may need to double-check it with a dictionary.
- Read some novel openings aloud in order to examine how professional writers select words and phrases to enhance meaning. Ask the children to isolate words or phrases that stand out to them as being good in some way.
- Write one or two on the board for closer examination. Ask them why it is a good sentence or phrase. Which particular words are working well? If the author had been having an off day, which less powerful words or phrasing might they have used instead?
- Tell them that, as young writers, a thesaurus will help them to create great choices in their writing.

Talk

- Write a story together on the board. Begin with a simple line such as, 'It was a hot day'. Ask the children to look up 'hot' to find some alternatives. Rework the sentence on the board.
- Then ask for a volunteer to provide the next simple sentence, ready for thesaurus work.

Curriculum objectives

- To use a thesaurus.

Success criteria

- I can look up new and alternative words using a thesaurus to enhance my writing.

Using a thesaurus

How do I use a thesaurus?

Learn

A thesaurus is a really useful tool. It helps you to find other words that have similar meanings to ones you are using. This means you don't have to use the same word twice.

A thesaurus is organised in alphabetical order, just like a dictionary. After that the words are arranged by the order of their second letter. Words that start with the same second letter are then arranged in the alphabetical order of their third letters and so on. It sounds complicated so here is an example from one section of a thesaurus. In this, all of the words begin with 'i'.

i**d**entity, i**m**mediate	in**d**ividual, in**t**erfere	inte**r**rupt, inte**s**tine
ordered by second letter	ordered by third letter	ordered by fifth letter

To start using a thesaurus, you just need to know what letter the word you want starts with. The more letters you know at the start of the word, the easier it is.

Checking meaning

A thesaurus is not a dictionary. They do different jobs. A thesaurus does not tell you what a word means. It only gives you words with similar meanings. These are called **synonyms**. However, because some words have more than one meaning, a thesaurus might give you words that don't fit into what you are writing.

Sometimes you need to check the meaning of some words in a dictionary to make sure you are using the right ones.

In this sentence the word **right** means correct.   That is the **right** answer.

✓ Tip

Looking up **right** in a thesaurus would give you: *correct, accurate, true, precise, just, proper, entitlement, privilege, permission* and lots more. You might have to look some of these words up in the dictionary to make sure you picked the best word.

If we try some of the words in the example sentence, they don't work.

That is the *privilege* answer – doesn't make sense.
That is the *precise* answer – makes sense.
So do *correct, accurate, true* and *proper*.

Try putting your new word in your sentence to see if it makes sense. Make sure the word you use fits with your meaning.

Activities

- Have dictionaries out as well so that when an uncommon word such as 'sweltering' comes up, it can be double-checked. Also, discuss the pros and cons of the class offerings to decide which one fits best – talk about subtle differences in meanings between the words.

- Use the activities in the textbook and on pages 46–47 of the *Year 6 Practice Book* to consolidate understanding.

- Extend activity 7 in the textbook by providing other commonly used words as a starter.

- Use a thesaurus to find synonyms for simple words, such as 'walk'. Demonstrate how the words found, such as 'amble', 'stroll', 'hike', 'march' and 'stride' all have subtle differences in the style or speed of walking. This could be done in a fun way by physically acting out the verbs.

Activities

1. Rewrite these words in the order you would find them in a thesaurus.

   | environment | existence | especially | exaggerate | equip | excellent | embarrass |

2. Choose one of the following words. Look up its synonyms in a thesaurus and write them down.

   | sacrifice | secretary | shoulder | signature |

3. Write a sentence using your chosen word from the question above. Then rewrite it using one of the words from your thesaurus.

4. Replace *conscience* in this sentence with a word from a thesaurus.

   Going to war was against his conscience.

5. Replace *familiar* in this sentence with a word from a thesaurus that shows Izzie always writes this way.

   Izzie signed the birthday card in her familiar style of handwriting.

6. Use a thesaurus to find another word to replace *familiar* in the same sentence. This time make it mean that Izzie is writing in an informal style.

7. Write as many words as you can think of that mean the same as *friend*. Use a thesaurus to check how many you got right.

8. A thesaurus sometimes gives you words that mean the opposite of the one you are using. These are called 'antonyms'. Use a thesaurus to find antonyms for: *ancient*, *definite*, *desperate*, *hindrance*, *individual*.

100 English Lessons Year 6 links:

- Starter activity 7 (page 12): Dictionary and thesaurus game
- Starter activity 17 (page 14): Synonyms and antonyms
- Autumn 1, Week 5 (page 33): Lesson 5, There and back again
- Spring 1, Week 1 (pages 83–85): explore goodies and baddies
- Spring 1, Week 6 (pages 98–100): draft a poem inspired by 'Jabberwocky'
- Summer 2, Week 4 (pages 188–190): write a modern street child story
- Summer 2, Week 6 (pages 194–196): compose a Victorian-style poem

Year 6 Practice Book links:

- (pages 46–47): Using a thesaurus

Identifying main ideas and Identifying key details

Prior learning

- Know how to skim and scan a text.

Learn

- Explain that identifying the main ideas and key details from a text will not only help the children to read faster for information, but also in structuring their own work.
- Read out a text, but don't tell the children the title. Their task is to listen to the sentences and try to guess the title, based on their assessment of the main idea.

Talk

- Provide a range of newspaper articles of two or three paragraphs in size, perhaps from a local newspaper. Having removed the headlines prior to the lesson, ask the children to work in pairs or small groups to discuss what the main ideas and key details are. Can they provide a headline?

Curriculum objectives

- To summarise the main ideas drawn from more than one paragraph, identifying key details that support the main ideas.

Success criteria

- I can draw together the main ideas and details to summarise a piece of writing.

Identifying main ideas

Learn

What does identifying main ideas mean?

The main ideas are the important things that the author wants the reader to know.

Often there will be only one main idea in a passage but there may be more than one paragraph.

Don't worry about each individual idea. Look for something that links them all.

In the passage below there is one main idea.

When you identify something, you find it in a passage. To find the main ideas, decide what a passage is about overall.

> The house at the end of our street is very spooky. It is painted black and has tall, thin chimneys. All of the windows are dark and no one ever seems to go in or out.

Each of the sentences is about something different but they are all about the spooky house at the end of the street, so this is the main idea.

✓ Tip

Try reading the text and then thinking of a **heading** that fits it overall.
- There are sentences on the colour of the house, what it looks like and who goes there. None of these is the main idea.
- Each sentence is about what makes the house spooky. So the title could be '**The Spooky House**'.

Activities

Highlight the words in each sentence that show what the sentence is about. Then find a link between them.

1. Read this passage and identify the main idea.

> People have always been fascinated by the moon. Is it made of cheese? What is on the other side of it? Can human beings live there? Modern science has answered many of these questions and we now know that there is much more to learn about the moon than we already know.

52 Reading

Activities

- Write an extra paragraph for 'The Spooky House' from page 52 of the textbook.
- Using the paragraph on how Hull has changed (page 53 of the textbook) as a model, ask the children to write a paragraph on how they have changed as a person through their life.
- Using the Menorca paragraph as a model, ask the children to construct a piece of writing around a holiday of their own. Tell them to decide what the main idea is before they start so that they can make sure the key details fit in with their main idea. Can their partner guess what their main idea was?

Write

- Ask the children to write a speech about an interest or hobby of their own. Tell them to give it a title in advance, but not to reveal this to anyone. Ask volunteers to deliver their speeches to the class, while the audience not only has the task of listening and enjoying, but also of listening to the key details to decide what the main idea is. Can they guess the actual title given by its author?

Identifying key details

What does identifying key details involve?

Learn

- Identify means find.
- The main ideas are the important things that the author wants the reader to know.
- The key details are what the author writes about the main ideas.

Start by identifying the main idea or ideas.

> The city of Hull sits proudly on the north bank of the River Humber. At one time, it was the biggest fishing port in the country but now its fishing fleet has disappeared. Nowadays, it is a modern city with fast motorway access and direct ferry links to Europe.

Main idea: how Hull has changed.

Next, highlight the points that tell us more about the main idea.

> The city of Hull sits proudly on the north bank of the River Humber. At one time, **it was the biggest fishing port in the country** but now **its fishing fleet has disappeared**. Nowadays, it is a **modern city** with **fast motorway access** and **direct ferry links to Europe**.

Each point tells us something different.

Now, use your highlighted points to give three ways that Hull has changed.

1. It is a modern city.
2. It has fast motorway access.
3. It has direct ferry links to Europe.

Activities

1. Read the passage below.

   > Last summer we had our best holiday ever. We went to Menorca and spent a week splashing about in the pool and on the beach. We laughed all day and never had to worry about going to bed late or getting up early. I made lots of new friends.

   a. What is the main idea?
   b. Give two key details from the text to support this:

Reading 53

---

100 English Lessons Year 6 links:

- Autumn 1, Week 3 (pages 25–27): summarise ideas from a story to use in diary writing
- Autumn 2, Week 2 (pages 54–56): analyse characters from *Alice in Wonderland*
- Spring 1, Week 3 (pages 89–91): take a look at allegory in *The Lion, the Witch and the Wardrobe*
- Summer 1, Week 2 (pages 150–152): write about 'home'
- Summer 1, Week 4 (pages 156–158): explore emotion and theme in *Carrie's War*
- Summer 1, Week 5 (pages 159–161): examine the events of Anne Frank's life
- Summer 1, Assess and review (page 166): *Carrie's War*
- Summer 2, Week 4 (pages 188–190): look at Jim's story from *Street Child*

Year 6 Practice Book links:

- (page 100–101): Beowulf, folk hero

Summarising main ideas

Prior learning

- Know how to skim and scan a text for main ideas and key details.
- Summarise stories in talk and writing.

Learn

- Explain that often a longer text can move from one main idea to another, particularly if it is offering a balanced argument upon a certain topic.
- Review the examples in the textbook.

Talk

- As a regular activity, ask the children to recommend recent books they've read. This can be done in groups or as a whole class with brave volunteers coming to the front. Tell them that when recommending a book with a story, it's a kind of summary, but you shouldn't give away too much about the middle or end of the book.

Curriculum objectives

- To summarise the main ideas drawn from more than one paragraph, identifying key details that support the main ideas.
- To recommend books that they have read to their peers, giving reasons for their choices.

Success criteria

- I can summarise different ideas from separate paragraphs within the same piece of writing.
- I can recommend a book I've read using a summarised review.

Summarising main ideas

Learn

What does summarising ideas mean?

Summarise means sum up. When you summarise, you say briefly what the passage is about.

A summary might be one word, a complete sentence or more than one sentence. You need to find ideas from the whole text.

You have to read the whole passage before you can summarise. In the passage below, there are different ideas for each paragraph.

> My sister Carly is very kind. She has a mischievous twinkle in her eyes. She is very popular and makes every day feel like a party.

Main idea: my sister Carly

> My other sister, Caroline, is very different. She is a very private person who prefers her own company. She has a good sense of humour but rarely uses it outside of the house.

Main idea: my sister Caroline

There are sentences about two sisters. The link between these two ideas (or paragraphs) are linked by the differences in the sisters.

When there is a lot of information in a passage, you might have to write more than one sentence as a summary.

The main idea in the following passage is healthy eating. The reasons that support healthy eating have been highlighted in blue and the reasons against it are in orange.

Healthy eating

Everybody loves food. Children love fast food. Burgers, chips and nuggets all taste great. There are lots of takeaway shops, meaning that fast food is easy to buy. It isn't always good for you though. Lots of fast food contains large amounts of salt and fat. Salads are really healthy but some people think that they are boring. Healthy eating gives us energy and makes us grow strong. However, if you're busy, a takeaway once in a while won't do you too much harm.

Activities

- Make wall charts for common errors.
- As an ongoing activity, have proofreading races. Provide texts with a set number of mistakes to spot. These could be differentiated to make the race fair. Include mistakes to do with spelling, verb tenses, punctuation, grammar and the use of Standard English.
- Use personal spelling books for the children to collect their own list of words to learn. If they are to be tested, let each learner pick their own set of 5, 10 or 20 spellings as a challenge and ask them to work in pairs to challenge each other – it's not about how many you get wrong, but how many you get right.

---

2. **This text contains a lot of verb errors. Rewrite it correctly.**

   > I am sat at my desk. I often thinks it's a great place for looks out of the window. Across the road is where my friend, Carl, lives. I seen him last night. I've known him since I been small. I call him on the phone last night but he's not answering.

3. **This text has lots of punctuation mistakes. Rewrite it with the correct punctuation.**

   > How do I explain newtons law of motion. There are lots of ways tell you show you do a demonstration. Whichever way i choose i know youll shout wow when I do?

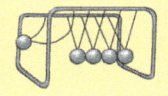

4. **This text has lots of different types of grammatical mistake. Rewrite it correctly.**

   > We meet before we went to the match. We runs quick to make sure catches the buses. The match was an boring game. After the game we have waited for the bus. The bus is slow. We got home very later.

5. **This text has lots of mistakes in the use of Standard English. Rewrite it in formal language.**

   > I ain't no fan of travelling. I dunno why folks rabbit on about it. There's an old geyzer near ours that reckons he's been every which where. It does me nut. IMHO home is best.

6. **This text has lots of different mistakes. Rewrite it without any of them.**

   > I ain't got no hang-ups about school. Why do sum people wurry about it. You goes. You gets good results and you ends up with a good job. Where's the prob. I like like school. When I'm sat in lessons I'm really happy.

---

100 English Lessons Year 6 links:

- Autumn 1, Week 5 (page 33): Lesson 4, Planning stories
- Spring 1, Week 5 (page 96): Lesson 2, Screenplay
- Spring 2, Week 1 (page 117): Lesson 4, Proofread and polish
- Summer 2, Week 2 (page 184): Lesson 5, Polishing the report
- Summer 2, Week 4 (page 190): Lesson 5, Modern street child
- Summer 2, Week 5 (page 193): Lesson 4, Writing Brunel's life

Answers Year 5

GRAMMATICAL WORDS

Page 7

1. **a.** The lazy <u>boy</u>; the difficult <u>piano piece</u>.
   b. The old, hungry <u>wolf</u>; the full <u>moon</u>.
   c. The <u>book</u> I'm reading at the moment; a group of teenage <u>sisters</u>.
   d. my brand new <u>pencil case</u> from Granny.
   e. The three lucky <u>ballet fans</u>; the Russian <u>ballet</u> in London.
   f. a fascinating <u>idea</u> in the bath.

2. Accept any answer which includes:
   a. mobile phone   **b.** diver/diving board
   c. spotty dress   **d.** ice cream

3. Accept any answers that expand these nouns:
   a. girls; house   **b.** man; mountain   **c.** Susan; journey; school
   d. John; noise   **e.** children; cake   **f.** lion; zebras

4. Accept any answers where the following nouns phrases have been changed:
   b. The Queen, who was loved by all; a magnificent palace surrounded by a forest
   c. The anxious parents; the silent exam hall
   d. The secondhand estate car a bitter disappointment

Page 9

1. **a.** Bonny has not practised enough for her violin exam.
   b. Sasha has trained very hard for the race.
   d. We have brought our wellie boots just in case.

2. **b.** Tilly had thought that playing a trick on Mrs Parker was a good idea.
   d. We had gone to the beach first.
   e. Mr Carter had forgotten the hockey sticks.

3. Example answers:
   a. Ow. That bee has stung me!
   b. The sun has risen over the fence.
   c. The major has presented an award to the firefighters for their bravery.
   d. Jude has won a writing competition.
   e. "Look! It has started to snow!"
   f. The ice skater has fallen and twisted her ankle.

4. Example answers:
   a. We had driven half way to Granny's when we realised we had forgotten the baby.
   b. Stephanie had tried to learn French.
   c. Manuel had finished when the bell went.
   d. Our money had run out so we decided to go home.
   e. We had washed the dishes and were ready to go.
   f. The balloon had drifted all the way to Australia.

Page 10

1. Example answers:
   a. May I go to the bathroom, please?
   b. We could go to the cinema this afternoon.
   c. They will be going on holiday on Saturday.

2. Sunita should tidy her bedroom.   Modal of possibility
   Sunita must tidy her bedroom.   Modal of certainty
   Sunita might tidy her bedroom.   Modal of possibility
   Sunita can tidy her bedroom.   Modal of certainty

Page 11

1. **a.** Opposite sides of a rectangle are obviously equal lengths.
   b. Maybe the water will be warm enough to swim in.
   c. There is probably enough petrol in the car.

2. Accept any correctly structured sentence that includes one of the following adverbs: probably, perhaps, maybe, certainly, definitely, obviously, clearly, possibly

Page 13

1. **a.** which we were listening to
   b. whose window it was
   c. where the game was to be played
   d. which Sophie had trodden on

2. **a.** the sofa   **b.** Josie   **c.** the girl   **d.** a joke

3. **a.** Look – that's the player <u>who</u> scored the goal.
   b. The volcano, <u>which</u> everyone thought was dormant, erupted.
   c. I can't find the book <u>that</u> I know I had yesterday.

4. **a.** Katerina, who is my new best friend, is coming to dinner.
   b. The corner shop, which has been closed for a refit, is opening tomorrow.
   c. The weather is lovely in Dubai, where I have been this week.
   d. We took care on the road, which was bumpy.

5. **a.** This is the new girl who I told you about.
   b. Paul has the book that Cameron lent me.
   c. Let's go to the shop that Finn told me about.
   d. We avoided the path that Granny fell over on last time.

PUNCTUATION

Page 15

1. **a.** It's time to go, silly.
   b. Please stop hitting Tamara.
   c. Sam loves cooking, animals and fast cars.
   d. Sam loves cooking animals and fast cars.
   e. It's time to go silly.
   f. Please stop hitting, Tamara.

2. Example answers:
   a. Tell your cousin whose name is Alex.
   b. Alex – tell your cousin.
   c. Shall we eat our friend called Donna?
   d. Donna – shall we eat?
   e. I made some decorations out of paper, which was silver-coloured, and glue.
   f. I used silver, as well as paper and glue, to make some decorations.

3. **a.** It's your turn to hide, Bunny.
   b. Julie, says my mother, should know better.
   c. The dog barked suddenly, hearing the doorbell ring.
   d. We bought some peanut butter, biscuits, chocolate milk and some apples.
   e. The teacher says Sophie is cross.

Page 17

1. **a.** Toby (a six-year-old collie dog) was lost for seven days.
   b. There are many ways, most of them difficult, to climb Mount Snowdon. Or There are many ways to climb Mount Snowdon, most of them difficult.
   c. 'Grab a piece of my heart' – such a great song – will be number one next week.
   d. My new book – *Wheelchair Warrior* – is going to be a best seller, according to my publisher. Accept commas/dashes the other way round.

2. Our favourite place is Venice.

Page 19

1. **a.** re-enact   **b.** co-own   **c.** co-opt   **d.** re-educate
   e. re-emphasise   **f.** re-energise   **g.** re-examining

2. **a.** re-elected   **b.** reclaim   **c.** re-emerge   **d.** re-enter
   e. disappear   **f.** re-covered   **g.** recover

178   Planning and Assessment Guide

3 a. The swimmers plunged into the ice-cold water.
   b. We ran out into the snow-covered garden.
   c. Kuba slowly saved up twenty-five pounds.
   d. Watch out – the iron is red-hot.
   e. We decided that the chocolate-coated raisins were one of our five-a-day.
   f. The cottage looked very run-down.
   g. My sister's bedroom is a definite no-go area.

Page 20

1 a. Explanation b. List c. Explanation d. List

2 a. Don't sit on the wall: the top bricks are loose.
   b. Practise both your piano pieces: 'Rowing boat' and 'Lullaby'.

3 Accept any reasonable wording following the colon in each sentence. Example answers:
   a. Mum didn't mind when John broke the vase: she didn't like it anyway!
   b. I have three things to do before school: get dressed, eat my breakfast and brush my teeth.
   c. Wednesday is my favourite day of the week: we have art and PE.

Page 21

1 a. There are three types of volcanoes:
- active volcanoes
- dormant volcanoes
- extinct volcanoes.

   b. Key facts about Michael Morpurgo:
- He has written over 100 books.
- He was Children's Laureate from 2003–2005.
- He runs a charity called 'Farms for City Children'.
- He is the author of War Horse.

2 Accept any reasonable answers in a bulleted list with correct punctuation.

VOCABULARY

Page 22

1 spell – misspell appoint – disappoint
   treat – mistreat approve – disapprove

2 a. misshapen b. disembark c. mismatch d. disbelieve

Page 23

1 a. overspend b. rearrange c. defrost

2 a. The spy decoded the message.
   b. We reclaimed our baggage after the flight.
   c. The car overtook us on the inside lane.

Page 24

1 a. originate b. medicate c. commentate

2 a. appreciate b. domesticate c. demonstrate

Page 25

1 a. The butter had started to solidify.
   b. The children were able to dramatise the story of Gelert.
   c. The farmer needed to fertilise his crops.

2 a. individualise b. quantify c. acidify d. terrorise

3 a. terrify b. popularise c. capitalise

Page 26

1 a. available b. considerable c. noticeable d. enjoyable

2 a. reliably b. understandably c. comfortably d. considerably

Page 27

1 a. force → forcible → forcibly
   b. incredulous → incredible → incredibly
   c. admission → admissible → admissibly
   d. comprehension → comprehensible → comprehensibly
   e. response → responsible → responsibly

Page 28

1 a. refer + ing → referring b. transfer + ed → transferred
   c. refer + e → referee d. prefer + ence → preference
   e. prefer + ing → preferring

SPELLING

Page 29

1 a. weight b. eighth c. achieve d. neighbour e. ceiling

2 a. weight b. mischievous c. neighbour

3 a. achieve b. thief c. perceive d. weight e. eight f. retrieve

Page 30

1 a. 'uff' sound: tough, enough
   'ow' sound: bough
   'oe' sound: although, though
   'or' sound: bought, fought, nought, thought
   b. trough

2 a. I thought I would be able to get there in time.
   b. The sea was very rough.
   c. We crawled through the tunnel.
   d. The boxers fought in the ring.
   e. Although it was very stormy, we managed to reach port.

Page 31

1 a. ya**c**ht b. i**s**land c. dou**bt** d. mus**c**le

2 a. They rowed the boat towards the deserted isle.
   b. I am going to write a story.
   c. The lamb was born just after its twin.
   d. Dad used the bread knife to cut me a slice.
   e. He cut his thumb on the glass.

Page 32

1 'cious' words: ferocious, gracious, spacious, vicious, atrocious, precious, suspicious, delicious
   'tious' words: ambitious, infectious, fictitious, superstitious, fractious, nutritious, cautious, scrumptious

2 a–d. Accept silly sentences that contain the target words.

3 a. The chocolate cake with sprinkles on it was completely scrumptious.
   b. The tennis player had a nutritious snack of nuts and banana before the match.
   c. When Abdul had chickenpox he had to stay away from school because he was infectious.
   d. My superstitious aunt is frightened of black cats.

4 a. The princess cried when she lost her precious diamond ring.
   b. My little cousin Oscar is very fractious when he is hungry.
   c. Scarlet was jealous of her sister's spacious new room.
   d. The movie star was very gracious when the girls asked for her autograph.

Page 33

1 president → presidential torrent → torrential
   office → official race → racial
   artifice → artificial commerce → commercial
   part → partial confident → confidential
   crux → crucial face → facial

2 a. Most sportsmen find it beneficial to warm up before exercising.
   b. The children in Year 5 are going on a residential course for a week.
   c. Fabio programmed the robot to perform a number of sequential movements.
   d. The doctor said that Abi's cut was superficial and only needed a plaster.
   e. My first initial is T (for Tamsin).
   f. Toby gets preferential treatment because he is the son of the headmaster.

3 **a.** Josh's little brother, Alfie, is our unofficial team mascot.
    b. Lucky Kuba has a substantial amount of Lego.
    c. It is antisocial to play your music too loud – it's also bad for your ears!
    d. My father, who is a spy, reads many confidential documents.
    e. It is essential, but very hard, to get a good night's sleep before an exam.
    f. Aikedo, Tae Kwon Do, Kung Fu and Karate are all martial arts.

Page 34

1 expectation → expectant   toleration → tolerance
   consequential → consequence   observation → observant
   confidential → confidence

2 **a.** Maddy tried to look innocent as she hid her phone under her homework.
    b. Cameron's frequent trips to the toilet made Mr Drake exasperated.
    c. The books we ordered at the recent book fair have arrived.

3 **a.** The fox waited by the entrance to the rabbit hole.
    b. The sailor's experience saved his life in the storm.
    c. "Silence at once!" shouted the teacher.

4 **a.** Seatoller has the highest frequency of rain in England.
    b. "At least have the decency to say sorry!" cried Jane.
    c. "Come quick!" called Dad, with great urgency in his voice.
    d. After Charlie left, there was a vacancy on the school council.

Page 35

1 **a.** I practised the piano every day.
    b. The bride walked up the aisle.
    c. I prepared the guest bedroom for the visitors.
    d. He walked straight past me.
    e. They're going on holiday next week.

Page 37

1 build – i sound: ui
   circle – s sound: c at beginning
   vehicle – h in the middle: difficult to hear
   relevant – e or a in middle, ant or ent
   parliament – ia in the middle
   environment – n before ment
   restaurant – or sound: au in the middle, ant or ent

2 **a.** calendar **b.** government **c.** twelfth
    d. dictionary **e.** business

3 **a.** vegetable **b.** regular **c.** separate **d.** recognise **e.** familiar

Page 39

1 **a.** crank, cricket, crinkle, crisp
    b. accident, animal, ant, antelope **c.** drill, drink, drip, drop

2 Page number will vary depending on the dictionary used.

3 Answers will depend on the dictionary used.

4 **a.** Accept any answer that means 'angry'.
    b. Accept any answer that means 'happy'.
    c. Accept any answer that means 'said'.
    d. Accept any answer that means 'walked'.

5 **a.** Accept is to take something when it is offered; except means 'not including'.
    b. Cross means 'angry' or 'bad-tempered'; mad is when you have something wrong with your mind.
    c. Stationery is paper, pens and other things you use for writing; stationary means 'not moving' or 'still'.
    d. Principle is a general truth, belief or rule; principal means 'chief' or 'most important'.

6 **a.** grass (glove – guitar)
    b. lizard (litter – long)
    c. low (look – lying)
    d. lock (litter – long)
    e. lorry (look – lying)

READING

Page 40

1 The dangers of motor racing.

Page 41

1 **a.** Weekends are wonderful.
    b. No school; no work; we can do what we want.

Page 42

1 My dad was annoyed by the cat's bad behaviour.
   My mother found the cat's behaviour amusing.

2 Dad's annoyed!

Page 43

1 Check the children's answers.

Page 45

1 **a.** On the north bank of the River Thames.
    b. Almost a thousand years ago.
    c. It had a gruesome reputation.
    d. The Crown Jewels.
    e. The Tower of London: has been a stronghold; has been frightening.

Page 47

1 **a.** For example, Caravans have to be set up when you arrive, whereas campervans do not require any setting up.
    b. For example, Caravans and campervans both have hot and cold running water.

2 **a.** 1970s: heavy metal, pop, glam rock; nowadays: hip hop, garage, house.
    b. In the 1970s music artists had individual talents which made them (and their music) memorable; nowadays music stars tend to be mass-produced to a standard formula which makes them easily forgettable.
    c. Record companies will always make more money than the stars they produce.

Page 49

1 The main theme is: bravery/courage

2 **a.** 'How would she ever find her way to the treasure now?'
    b. Searching for treasure is one of the conventions of an adventure story, with various obstacles needing to be overcome along the way.
    c. There are two frightening situations described in the extract: first, the danger of being swept away by the river and secondly, the scary prospect of being alone in the dark woods with no light.

Page 51

1 Mount Rushmore National Memorial is one of the most amazing sculptures ever made. (Opinion)
   The memorial was carved into the granite face of Mount Rushmore in South Dakota. (Fact)
   The project ran out of money. (Fact)
   Such a sculpture will never be achieved again. (Opinion)

2 Example answer:
    a. The sculpture was started in 1927.
    a. There are four heads of presidents carved into the stone.
    b. Only the heads were completed.

3 'It was a hard choice!'

Page 53

1 Example answers:
    a. She is feeling upset.
    b. She had 'a worried look on her face'.
    c. I think it was bad.
    d. If it had been a good report she would not have had a worried look on her face and she would not have hidden it under her pillow.

Page 54

1 charged = raced

2 'In vain' means that the writer ultimately wasn't successful in trying to make it back to the cliff.

Page 55

1. deter = discourage
2. The subsequent sentence explains that despite the distance tourists still go there. 'Help', 'disillusion' and 'exhaust' would not make sense in this context.

Page 57

1. **a.** 'Everyone'
   b. Because the way the sentence is written makes you think the statement must be true, and you wouldn't be 'normal' if you didn't actually like chocolate.
   c. The words all sound enticingly tasty and make you want to try eating the Chocolate Milkshake bar yourself.
2. **a.** 'A chill wind sliced…'; 'no place to be in the dark'.
   b. This is a rhetorical question which casts doubt in the mind of the reader as to whether ghosts might exist after all.
   c. Tension is built through the use of short sentences, as well as rhetorical questions to excite the reader's interest as to what Amy might have seen.
   d. The setting in the graveyard, the chill wind, the strange movement in the ground, the possibility of ghosts.

Page 59

1. **a.** Simile
   b. 'pools of pain' or 'steel spears'
   c. Figurative language:
   - 'it hid the teardrops that were swimming from my eyes': personification (teardrops can't actually swim)
   - 'in pools of pain': alliteration (repetition of the /p/ sound attracts attention to the words)
   - 'I stumbled home like a blind man': simile (use of this simile reinforces the previous sentences describing the writer's teardrops and trouble in seeing properly)

Page 60

1. Language:
   - Short sentences (On your own? Alone?)
   - Repetition of words (Would you go out in a graveyard in the dark? Would you go out in a haunted graveyard in the dark?)
   - Rhetorical questions (Are you brave? Or stupid?)
   Structural:
   - Heading (Do You Think You're Brave?)
   Presentational
   - Bold text (Do You Think You're Brave)

Page 61

1. The third-person style of writing draws the reader into the story. The writer appears to be addressing the reader directly, as if they were speaking face to face. This makes the reader feel more engaged, as if they were actually there experiencing the scary situation themselves.
2. The writer builds up tension through very short sentences, plus using an appropriately sinister simile.

Page 62

1. Example answers:
   a. What does 'welter' mean?
   b. When did the events in the story take place?
   c. Where were Torak and his father camping?
   d. What if Torak also gets attacked by the bear?
   e. I wonder what will happen to Torak's father.

Page 63

1. Example answers:
   a. 'Welter' means a state of general confusion.
   b. The events in the story took place the previous day [yesterday].
   c. Torak and his father were camping in the woods.
   d. I predict that Torak will escape from the bear. Maybe he will be able to hide in the woods and return to the camp as soon as the bear has gone.
   e. I think that with Torak's help his father will recover from his injury.

2. Children's own answers. Look for sensible, well-written questions.
3. Children's own answers. Look for sensible, well-written answers to the questions the children devised in activity 2.

WRITING

Pages 64–65

1. **a.** 'Lost' notice to be pasted on a shop window or lamp post, to be read by anyone walking past. (Short notes without full sentences, containing essential details only.)
   b. Recipe (numbered points, instruction text, brief to-the-point details).
   c. Newspaper or magazine article (heading, full details relating to who, what and when, quotes from people interviewed).
2. Check the children's piece of writing.
3. **a.** Thank-you letter: formal language, full sentences, polite tone.
   b. Postcard: informal language, jokey tone, brief sentences or notes.
   c. Instruction text: simple language, brief sentences or notes, friendly tone.
   d. News article: formal language, full sentences, interesting and relevant information.

Page 66

1. Children's own answers. Look for sensible choices for headings and subheadings.

Page 67

1. **a.** Omar and Ranvir eat their lunch and go out to play. or Omar and Ranvir ate their lunch and went out to play.
   b. The dog was barking loudly when the postman brought a letter.
   c. They were having their tea when the phone rang.
   d. The frog hopped off the lily pad into the water and swam away.
   e. The sun went behind the cloud and it was suddenly cold. or The sun goes behind the cloud and it is suddenly cold.
   f. I heard a car screech to a halt so I dashed to the window.

Page 69

1. **a.** Can you help me find my lost hat. It is red and I left it on the bench.
   b. Every time we tried to throw the smelly stick away, our dog went and fetched it.
   c. "Thanks for the tea. You can put it there."
   d. "Take your shoes off. They are covered in mud."
   e. The cat slept by the fire. It always slept by the fire in the afternoon.
2. Accept any appropriate conjunction.

Page 79

1. **Hare** zoomed off through the **wood**, down the lane and into the field and stopped just before the finish line. Next to the path, he saw a boulder looking warm in the **sun** and he suddenly felt sleepy.
2. "Tortoise is so far behind," he **thought**. "I'll sit on this warm rock and wait for Tortoise. Then I'll run off again so he can see me win." He lay down in the sun and **was** soon snoring. He slept as Tortoise plodded through the wood. He slept as Tortoise plodded down the lane and he slept as Tortoise plodded through the field. He **woke** up just in time to see Tortoise cross the finish line.
3. Once upon a time**,** there was a shepherd boy who spent his days alone on the hills guarding the sheep. It was very dull and he was very lonely. Every day he looked at the same wall**,** the same grass and the same sheep. What would happen, he wondered, if I shouted **"Wolf"**?
4. Before he knew what he was doing**,** he was shouting **"Wolf!"** and bashing **two** rocks together. All at once, the villagers **came** running. He was praised for his quick thinking and fussed over by his mother. It made a **great** change from his normal, boring day. The next day, the young shepherd **was** back in the field: same wall, same grass, same sheep.

Answers Year 6

GRAMMATICAL WORDS

Page 7

1. Accept any reasonable answer, for example:
   Some **grey baby** rabbits.
2. Accept any reasonable answer, for example:
   The church **behind** the school.
3. Accept any reasonable answer that follows the example.
4. Accept any reasonable answer, for example:
   A blonde haired film star with shiny teeth.
5. Accept any reasonable answer that contains three expanded noun phrases, for example:
   The young, ginger-haired boy searched his untidy bedroom but could not find his favourite story book.
6. Accept any reasonable answer that contains three expanded noun phrases.

Page 8

1. a. He **has gone** out to play.
   b. They **have developed** a method for baking perfect bread.
2. I **had enjoyed** the film until the end spoiled it.

Page 9

1. Accept any reasonable answer, for example:
   a. The hotel, **which we liked**, was next to the beach.
   b. August, **when it is school holidays**, is very busy.
2. a. Relative clause b. Subordinate clause c. Main clause

Page 10

1. We could stay in on Saturday night but we might go to the cinema instead.
2. George **must/should/ought** to improve his backhand if he wants to win the tennis match.
3. Emma will buy some jeans on Saturday.

Page 11

1. Accept any reasonable answer, for example:
   a. It is definitely six miles to town.
   b. I can possibly come to see you later.
   c. Maybe we can have tea together.
2. Accept any appropriate explanation, for example:
   'Clearly' suggests they expect to win.
   'Possibly' suggests some doubt about whether they will win.

Page 13

1. a. My mum drove the car. b. Our cat ate its food.
2. a. Dad is making tea. b. The dog chased the cat.
3. a. Subject: You. Object: your bike.
   b. Subject: Sadie. Object: shoes.
   c. Subject: Ronny. Object: his motorbike.
   d. Subject: Mrs Burman. Object: her school.
4. Accept any answers that include subjects and objects used correctly, for example:
   d. 'Cara, my best friend, sings songs.' is acceptable. 'Cara, my best friend, sings loudly.' is not because 'loudly' is an adverb and is not the subject of the verb.

Page 15

1. a. A wonderful meal was made by the chef.
   b. The criminal was arrested by the police officer.
   c. Our car was mended by a mechanic.
   d. A letter was sent by my cousin to the Pope. Or A letter was sent to the Pope by my cousin.
   e. A boat was rowed across the Atlantic Ocean by four mums from Yorkshire in 2016. Or A boat was rowed across the Atlantic Ocean in 2016 by four mums from Yorkshire.
2. a. Everyone had a good time.
   b. The runner smashed the world record.
   c. Torrential rain has caused terrible floods. Or Torrential rain caused terrible floods.
   d. A massive hurricane has destroyed many homes in America. Or In America, a massive hurricane has destroyed many homes. Or A massive hurricane destroyed many homes in America.
   e. The fire brigade has rescued our cat from a tree. Or The fire brigade rescued our cat from a tree.
3. a. Passive b. Active c. Passive d. Active e. Active

Page 17

1. a. It is important that you **be** on time for the show.
   b. If I **were** you, I would take the risk.
2. a. If I were b. be quieter
3. a. If Zoe **were** to play instead of Zena, we would win easily tonight.
   b. It is important that you **be** here on time.
   c. I wish it **were** Saturday.
   d. If only my car **were** more reliable.
   e. It is essential that pupils **be** polite.
   f. I advise that you **be** present at the hearing.
   g. Dr Lazarus asked that the patient **wait** outside.
   h. Chaz requested that Ziggy **come** to his party.
   i. It is essential that the referee **be** allowed to control the game.

PUNCTUATION

Page 18

1. a. My mum loves cooking, my dad and me.
   b. Nate invited two boys, John and Eddy.
   c. My uncle, a singer and a dancer, often appeared on television.
   d. Has the cat eaten, Callum?

Page 19

1. a. You won't be late, <u>will you</u>?
   b. We're going to the cinema, <u>aren't we</u>?
2. a. You'd like pizza for tea, **wouldn't you**?
   b. This is the right answer, **isn't it**?

Page 20

1. My mother-in-law is coming for Sunday lunch.
2. My uncle, a retired surgeon, showed me some of his little-used instruments.
3. re-sign

Page 21

1. a. Morgan's Magic Medicine:
   - Good for young and old alike
   - Will cure your aches and pains
   - It works quickly
   - No after-effects
   - It comes in handy half-litre bottles
   - Available from all good chemists

182 Planning and Assessment Guide

b. Stop and Go bike locks:
- Handy and little locks
- Fit to the front wheel of a bike
- Work automatically every time you stop
- They are so simple
- No need for keys or codes
- Flick the switch and you're off again

Page 22

a. You will need to bring with you: your passport, plane tickets, money, sun cream and sunglasses.
b. We now know some countries that border the Mediterranean Sea: Egypt, France, Spain and Italy.
c. Warm waters can be found in: the Mediterranean Sea, the Caribbean Sea and the Indian Ocean.

2   I need to go to: the supermarket for dog, cat and fish food; the heel bar to get my shoes, boots and sandals mended; and the library to get some books for my history project.

Page 23

3   **a.** The manager looked around the dressing room and said, "Some of you were useless last week, so for this week the defence will be: Smith, Brown, Martin, Culshaw and Blair. In midfield I'm having: Middleton, Sutton, Mason, Devlin. Up front it will be: Nagla and Hussain."
b. To succeed in life you need a lot of things: talent, determination, hard work and a lot of luck.

4   **a.** I have been learning Spanish on the internet for three weeks. Already I can: tell people my name; book a room; order drinks at the bar; and explain that I do not understand a word they are saying.
b. I have bought all of the birthday presents for my family early this year. For my sister I have a camera and a memory card; a box of expensive chocolates; and a day at a spa. My mother is getting an imitation diamond necklace; two tickets to the cinema, so she can take me as well; and some chocolates. My brother is getting nothing because he is always mean to me; never does his share of the washing up; and plays Taylor Swift at full volume while I am trying to watch television.

5   **a.** The head teacher looked at the boy and said, "Let's have a look at your attendance record. This is what you have done this week: Monday: morning absent; afternoon late. Tuesday: late in the morning; absent in the afternoon. Wednesday: absent morning; absent afternoon. Need I go on?"
b. "From now on it's going to be like this: You will attend school every day; be on time; and make sure you are wearing your full uniform. Is that too much to ask?"

Page 24

1   **a.** Full marks in the test again: just what I expected.
b. Paris is a beautiful city: you can see many famous sights there.
c. Martin didn't want to sell his car: he needed the money he would get for it.
d. The sky looks dark: it will rain heavily all day.
e. I love Skiathos: I am really looking forward to going there on holiday again.

2   Accept any appropriate independent clauses that add to the first one in each case, for example:
a. I know exactly what I want for my birthday: a green bike with a bell and basket.

Page 25

3   **a.** My homework is due in tomorrow: I'll have to make sure I do it tonight.
b. I was ten last year; this year I'll be eleven.
c. I didn't do well in the spelling text this morning: there were some difficult words in it.
d. Who dares wins: who doesn't dare loses.
e. America is in the west; Russia is in the east.

4   Accept any appropriate explanation.

5   It separates two independent clauses. The second clause gives more information about the first. A colon is needed because the two clauses are not of equal importance.

6   **a.** Watch what you're doing – you could have had my eye out!
b. The postman has just delivered a parcel I ordered; I was expecting it.
c. Don't put it there – put it there!
d. There is a really interesting programme about China on television tonight; it is the kind of thing I like to watch.
e. All of my friends have phones; everybody uses them.

7   **c.** The road is difficult – it's almost impassable – you'll need a strong vehicle.
Reason: The dashes separate out the independent clauses.

Page 27

1   **a.** The three men (they looked like spies to me) talked quietly in the corner of the cafe.
b. Denny, my older brother, is joining the army.
c. Suki – a long-haired Alsatian – won first prize at the dog show.
d. I had to keep very still while the doctor, who was very gentle, took my stitches out. (Accept dashes or brackets in place of the commas.)
e. A massive hurricane – the strongest wind ever – will hit this country, probably on Tuesday next week. *Or* A massive hurricane, the strongest wind ever, will hit this country – probably on Tuesday next week.

VOCABULARY

Page 29

1

Word beginning	'ent' or 'ant'
observ	observant
innoc	innocent
toler	tolerant
obedi	obedient

2   **a.** buoyancy **b.** hesitancy **c.** agency
d. accountancy **e.** consistency

3   **a.** The non-**existence** of dodos in Mauritius has long been a cause for regret.
b. Your help is more of a **hindrance**.
c. Please complete the **relevant** application form.

4   Accept any appropriate sentences.

5   Accept any appropriate attempt at identifying words with the listed word endings from a fiction book.

Page 30

1   re — loyal — disloyal
dis × judge — misjudge
mis × design — redesign

2   replace, miscalculate, distasteful

Page 31

1   **a.** The doctor was **referring** him to a specialist.
b. The head teacher wrote a glowing **reference**.

2   **a.** inferred, inference   **b.** differing, difference
c. transferred, transference

Page 32

1   complex ✓   arduous ✓   intricate ✓

2   ancient — antique
curious × known
familiar × genuine
sincere × inquisitive

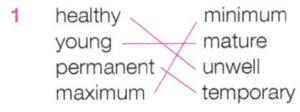

Page 33

1   healthy — minimum
young × mature
permanent × unwell
maximum — temporary

2   Accept any appropriate antonyms, for example:
a. I **destroyed** a massive tower.
b. The successful man was very **arrogant**.
c. The **sensible** child had no packed lunch.

Page 35

1. Formal vocabulary: a reply to a wedding invitation, a presentation to your class, a telephone bill.
   Informal vocabulary: a shopping list, a phone call to a friend, a postcard to your sister from your holiday.

2. Accept any appropriate answers, for example:

Formal vocabulary	Informal vocabulary
commence	start
conclude	end
renovate	do up
beverage	drink

3. Accept any appropriate answer, for example:
   Sonny: Good evening Tezza, it is Sonny.
   Tezza: Good evening Sonny. How can I help you?
   Sonny: Have you completed the homework? It is very difficult.
   Tezza: No. I plan to do it later. There is an extremely interesting programme on the television which I intend to watch first.
   Sonny: Please could you phone me back when you have completed the homework? I will have a short rest and then will try to complete it.

4. Accept any reasonable answers.
5. Accept any reasonable answers.
6. Accept any reasonable explanations.

SPELLING

Page 36

1. a. They **sought** a way out of the forest, but it was hard to find.
   b. I **brought** some toys with me.
   c. They installed a new **wrought** iron gate.
   d. We **bought** some cakes to have with our sandwiches.

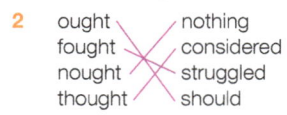

2. ought — nothing
   fought — considered
   nought — struggled
   thought — should

Page 37

1. a. They **roughly** worked out how to make the model.
   b. The doors were made of **toughened** glass.
   c. We bought some **doughnuts** to eat at the fairground.

2. area – borough   branch – bough
   cultivate – plough   sufficient – enough
   animal food container – trough

Page 38

1. a. They went over the bridge to the I<u>s</u>le of Anglesey.
   b. Look at the third colum<u>n</u>.
   c. We are inde<u>b</u>ted to you, thanks to all your efforts.
   d. Caitlin saw a mis<u>t</u>le thrush in the garden.

2. a. doubt   b. isle   c. condemn   d. bristle

Page 39

1. a. I went **twice** to call on Ahmed.
   b. There was a very **fierce** dog behind the gate.
   c. It was **bliss** sitting in the hot sun.
   d. Our teacher **suggested** that we read books by Michael Morpurgo.

2. a. practice   b. piece

Page 40

1. a. malicious, infectious, spacious, nutritious
   b. Accept any appropriate sentences.

2. a. cautious   b. suspicious   c. delicious   d. conscientious

Page 41

1. Accept correct spellings of: torrential, artificial, martial.
2. Accept correct spellings of: official, social and potential.

3. Accept any appropriate attempt at identifying and sorting the words under **tial** and **cial** headings.

Page 42

1. admirable, measurable, tolerable, dependable
2. enjoyably, changeably, reliably, reasonably
3. The 'y' is dropped and replaced by an 'i' and then 'able' or 'ably' is added.

Page 43

1. legible, legibly   sensible, sensibly
   reversible, reversibly   defensible, defensibly

2. Accept any appropriate answers, for example:
   a. The burnt pie was inedible.   b. His writing was illegible.

3. Accept any appropriate answers, for example:
   a. The burglars had **forcibly** entered the property.
   b. The child was **incredibly** upset after the fall.

Page 44

1. a. I searched everywhere for the **receipt** so I could return the faulty game.
   b. The **ceiling** was very uneven and would need plastering.
   c. The team finally **conceived** a plan which would help them win the tournament.
   d. Jack **received** a parcel on his birthday.

2. a. weigh   b. deceive   c. field
   d. perceive   e. neighbour   f. conceited

3. a. When ei is used after c it makes an /**ee**/ sound, e.g. receipt.
   b. When ei is not used after the letter c, it makes an /**ay**/ sound, e.g. weigh.

Page 45

1. a. imme**dia**tely double **m**; **iat**; is there an end **e** before **y**?
   b. **necessary** one **c** but double **s**; soft **s** made with **c**.

2. a. government   b. marvellous   c. recognise

Page 47

1. a. We <u>heard</u> the firework display in the park.
   b. I wondered <u>whose</u> car was parked outside my house.
   c. The burglar tried to <u>steal</u> the television, but it was very heavy.
   d. The porridge was <u>too</u> hot!

2. Accept any sentence using each homophone, for example:
   a. My sister **passed** her driving test.
   You need to meet me at half **past** three.
   b. We **guessed** that you wouldn't arrive until late.
   I helped mum prepare the **guest** bedroom.

3. a. aloud: to say something out loud; allowed: to have permission.
   b. farther: beyond, at a distance; father: dad.
   c. waste: rubbish/not making the best of something; waist: middle of your body, between chest and hips.

4. a. grate   b. descent   c. serial   d. bridle

Page 49

1. achieve, bargain, category, definite, embarrass, frequently, government, language, necessary, rhyme

2. accommodate, amateur, cemetery, committee, correspond, determined, dictionary, marvellous, mischievous, recommend, restaurant, rhythm

3. neat, necessary, need, needle, neither, neon, nest, net, nettle, network, never, newer

4. distract

5. circle, service, circus, survive, cease, siren

6. farewell, neither, piece, tomorrow ✓
   mischievious, neccessary, neice ✗

7. a. I will be going away next **week**.
   I will have to sit down as I am feeling **weak**.
   b. I have to sit down as I am feeling **faint**.
   He made a **feint** move that sent me in the wrong direction.
   c. That is not **allowed**.
   Don't speak **aloud**.

184   Planning and Assessment Guide

8 Accept a reasonable attempt to identify the different meanings of hand, both in noun and verb form, and an appropriate sentence, for example:
The second **hand** of the clock tells us how many minutes have past the hour.
My **hand** hurt when I trapped it in the door.
A **hand** is a unit of measurement for measuring the height of a horse.

Page 51

1 embarrass, environment, equip, especially, exaggerate, excellent, existence

2 Accept any appropriate listing of the words' synonyms.

3 Accept any appropriate sentences and those that work with a synonym exchanged for the original word, for example:
He had to **sacrifice** playing football in the evening so that he could get his homework finished in time for school the next morning.
He had to **forgo** playing football in the evening so that he could get his homework finished in time for school the next morning.

4 Accept any appropriate synonym, for example:
Going to war was against his **principles**.

5 Accept any appropriate synonym, for example:
Izzie signed the birthday card in her **usual** style of handwriting.

6 Accept any appropriate synonym, for example:
Izzie signed the birthday card in her **casual** style of handwriting.

7 Accept any appropriate synonyms for 'friend'.

8 Accept any appropriate antonyms for the words.

READING

Page 52

1 What we know about the moon.

Page 53

1 **a.** Last year's holiday to Menorca.
b. Accept any two from:
1. We spent a week in the pool and on the beach.
2. We never had to worry about going to bed late or getting up early.
3. Lots of new friends.

Page 55

1 **a.** Types of takeaway shops. **b.** Favourite takeaway meals.

2 Saturday night takeaway

3 Summary: My mother paints great landscapes but she is not as good at painting portraits.

Page 57

1 **a.** The public. **b.** Over one hundred years.
c. It was described as unsinkable. **d.** continuous

2 Titanic
/ \
Sea creatures now live in it.   There are memorials in five cities.

Page 59

1 **a.** Accept any one from:
Owls hop and penguins walk.
Penguins can swim, owls can't.
Owls can fly, penguins can't.
b. The way they move (graceful) or where they live (in the wild). Accept specific details.

2 **a.** The author would let a cat slide onto their knee but would not do the same with a snake.
b. Cats and snakes both hiss and spit. They both hunt small animals.
c. Cats are almost universally liked while snakes are hated the world over.

Page 61

1 myths and dragons

2 **a.** Possible answers: Dorca the dragon, quest, secret of eternal dragon life, knights of Nemore, dragon magic
b. Each phrase has stereotypical elements of myths.
c. Accept any two from: flying dragons, knights, quests and magic.

Page 63

1 **a.** fact **b.** opinion **c.** opinion **d.** fact

2 The *Mona Lisa* was painted by Leonardo da Vinci. It is also called *La Gioconda*. It is in the Louvre in Paris.

3 Accept any three from: The statue of *Venus de Milo* is much more impressive. It's not worth queuing to see the *Mona Lisa*. You'd be better off spending your time in the Egyptian section. The sphinx in there is really impressive.

Page 65

1 **a.** Accept scared, worried, apprehensive or similar.
b. 'Ella went as slowly as she could into the hall' or 'She wished she had been ill that morning'.
c. No
d. 'She wished she had practised more' shows she has not done enough work to do well. 'The test papers were lying menacingly on the desks' suggests that she feels threatened by them.

Page 67

1 **a.** The pupils are all safe outside the building. The fire brigade comes and puts out the fire.
b. These are the next logical steps from the clues in the passage.

2 **a.** He might congratulate her on saving all of the pupils and the teacher, or he might want to question her about how the fire started or how she found it.
b. Congratulate: She has saved the school. She did the correct things. She didn't panic when the fire alarm didn't work.
Question: His tone was serious. She was 'interviewed'. It took place in the head teacher's office. She was alone when she found the fire. The fire alarm didn't work at first.

Page 68

1 climbed

Page 69

1 hate
Explanation: The first sentence says the writer does not like rice pudding. The final sentence says the writer avoids it. 'Hate' is the only word that would fit with these two sentences.

Page 71

1 **a.** Exercise can make us healthier; help us live longer; help us feel better; help us to reduce weight.
b. Accept two from: walk, jog, run or swim.
c. Cheap – indicates that exercise need not be expensive. Huge – indicates amount of difference. Both words are meant to persuade the reader to exercise.

2 **a.** 'Run!' makes the reader feel as if they are being given the instruction. The repetition emphasises how important it is to run. It makes the passage scary because you do not know why you are running.
b. It emphasises the need to run because your life is in danger if you don't.
c. It increases the tension because it warns you but it doesn't tell you what is there. It increases the excitement because it makes you feel that whatever is chasing you is right behind you. It makes it seem like whatever is there is too scary to look at.

Page 73

1. **a.** a simile

   b.

Language used	Type of language and effect
Tears **burned** my eyes	This is a metaphor showing the heat of the tears.
held me **like a nurse**	The simile shows how the mother cared for the writer until he was well again.
My father brought the **remedy – superglue**.	This is a metaphor. The superglue acts like a medicine to cure everything.

Page 74

1.
Feature	Feature name	Example
Language	rhetorical question	Why had she hit the *send* button?
Structural	heading	Why oh why?
Presentational	italics	*send*

Page 75

1. **a.** It enables the reader to see and hear everything as if they were there. They are able to know what Sara is thinking.
   b. It leaves the passage on a cliffhanger. The reader does not know what Lewis's text will say but they can guess from what has gone before.

Page 77

1. **a.** The Great Train Robbery took place in 1963.
   b. A gang of robbers stopped the mail train from Glasgow to London by changing the signal to red.
   c. They took 120 sacks from the train.

2. There was £2 million on the train or there was a lot of money on the train.

3. Other people might be put off repeating their actions.

4. We will learn about our past.
   We might learn about our future.

WRITING

Page 79

1. **a.** People all over the country who need to know about the weather
   b. Mainly pupils in school. Also parents and teachers.
   c. Parents of children in school next year.
   d. Car drivers with unreliable cars. People who do not have much money.

2. Any answer that is planned and structured is acceptable. Reasons for choosing the writing style should explain why it fits the intended readership.

Page 81

1. Heading: **Accident on A59** or similar. Subheading: **Damage** or similar.

2. Second paragraph begins: Beneath the waves. This is because the previous text is generally about the activity but this paragraph is all about being underwater. Headings should summarise the passage, e.g. **Swimming on the Great Barrier Reef**. Subheadings should summarise the second paragraph, e.g. **Below the waves** or similar.

3. Accept any answers that include an appropriate bullet-pointed list, two paragraphs, appropriate heading and subheading (with reasonable explanations for their choice).

4. Answers should explain the reasoning of the three most important points with appropriate alternative headings.

Page 83

1. Tom met Katy at the school gate. She had done her homework but he hadn't. They decided that he had time to do it in the breakfast club.

2. Accept any conjunctions that make sense, for example:
   I wanted to go to the cinema but I couldn't because I didn't have enough money.

3. Accept any adverbial that shows time has passed, for example:
   The teacher watched the class leave the room. Shortly afterwards, the next class arrived at the door.

4. Accept any adverbial that shows the place has changed, for example:
   Emily looked out of the window. In the street, she could see the traffic passing by.

5. Accept any reasonable answer that includes all three adverbials in any order, for example:
   After school, I ran as quickly as I could to meet my friend at the end of the street.

6. Discussion should be about how Churchill repeats 'the beginning' and 'the end' linking them to show how things have changed.

Page 84

1. **a.** My son was born <u>at the start of this century</u>, in 2001. *Or* My son was born at the start of this century, <u>in 2001</u>.
   b. I went because I wanted to <u>go</u>.
   c. My sister likes salad but I don't <u>like salad</u>.

2. **a.** "**No** we don't."
   b. "**Yes** I have."
   c. "My dad **does**."

3. Answers should identify unnecessary words and suggest alternatives.

Page 85

1. "I saw a bird in the garden." *Or* "I have seen a bird in the garden."

2. Amy **has accompanied** Jack to the concert.

3. I **may/might/can/could/should/ought** to win the 100 metres race on Sports Day.

Page 86

1. The Tower of London, home to over 20,000 crown jewels, was built nearly 1000 years ago. It was a prison, a place of execution up until 1942 and has housed a royal zoo. Ravens are the only animals there now. It is said that if they leave, the kingdom will fall.

Page 87

1. If Sahid is late: Sahid is always late when he meets Tom at the park.
   If Tom is late: Tom is always late when he meets Sahid at the park.
   There may be other alternatives. Accept any answer that clearly identifies who is late.

2. Accept any answers that enhance the description.

3. Improvements to the piece of writing should focus on the effect of new words.

Page 89

1. The description table and continuation of the story should contain appropriate vocabulary and description for creating the setting and atmosphere.

2. The similes and metaphor should be clearly distinguishable and relevant to a description of a school.

3. Answers should expand on the description in the style of the example from page 88.

4. Discussion should focus around reasoning of the description choices and how to improve.

5. The final descriptions should show appropriate changes and improvements.

186 Planning and Assessment Guide

Page 91

1. The description table should contain appropriate vocabulary for a spy.
2. The paragraph should use examples from the description table.
3. The description table should describe a completely different spy.
4. The paragraph should describe the new character effectively.
5. The final paragraphs should show changes to vocabulary and punctuation, including the use of metaphors and similes.

Page 93

1. In our house there are six of us: my parents, my gran, my sisters and me. We have lived here for a long time. It was originally my grandparents' house. Nobody knows how long they lived here but it was over sixty years. Or similar.
   Acceptable alternative:
   - In our house there are six of us:
   - my parents
   - my gran
   - my sisters
   - me
   - Appropriate heading: Our house, The history of our house or similar.

2. **Alternatives table**

	Original	Alternatives
1.	It lie in the Caribbean Sea	Subject/verb agreement
2.	not far from Florida; or the rest of America or Europe but a long way from Alaska.	Not clear. Needs shortening to make main point clear.
3.	People who live three are called Cubans.	Spelling error
4.	It is much bigger than people who have never been there think that it is.	Too long. Needs shortening to make main point clear.
5.	The main cities are Havana Varadero Santiago de Cuba and Santa Clara.	Punctuation error. Needs colon and commas inserting.

   Possible edit:
   Cuba is a magical island. It lies in the Caribbean Sea. It is not far from Florida but a long way from Alaska. People who live there are called Cubans. It is much bigger than people think. The main cities are: Havana, Varadero, Santiago de Cuba and Santa Clara.
   Or similar. Accept bullet points for the final list.

3. Pupils should identify areas for changes in their partner's work and then make suggestions for improvements.

Page 94

1. My father once told me that I would never find my fortune without a lot of hard work. I spent the rest of my life trying to prove him wrong. I didn't manage it. I eventually had to admit that he was right.
   The spellchecker should not pick up *write* or *farther* as being the wrong spelling in this context.

Page 95

2. I am sitting at my desk. I often think it's a great place for looking out of the window. Across the road is where my friend, Carl, lives. I saw him last night. I've known him since I was small. I called him on the phone last night but he did not answer.

3. *Either:*
   How do I explain Newton's Law of Motion? There are lots of ways: tell you; show you; do a demonstration. Whichever way I choose I know you'll shout, "Wow!" when I do.
   Or:
   How do I explain Newton's Law of Motion? There are lots of ways:
   - tell you
   - show you
   - do a demonstration
   Whichever way I choose I know you'll shout, "Wow!" when I do.

4. We met before we went to the match. We ran quickly to make sure we caught the bus. The match was a boring game. After the game we waited for the bus. The bus was slow. We got home very late.

5. I do not like travelling. *(Or similar)* I do not know why people talk so much about it. There is an old man who lives near our house who thinks that he has been everywhere. It drives me mad. *(Or similar)* In my honest opinion home is best.

6. I don't have any problems with school. Why do some people worry about it? You go; you get good results; and you end up with a good job. Where's the problem? I like school. When I'm sitting in lessons I'm really happy.

Notes

Notes

SCHOLASTIC

National Curriculum
ENGLISH

A new whole-school primary English programme

- A complete English toolkit for teachers: **planning, assessment, textbooks, practice activities and ready-made lesson plans**
- Cost-effective **with no expensive subscription fees or repeat costs**
- Flexible and supportive **planning resources that will save teachers time**
- **Accessible and engaging content, fully matched to the English curriculum in England**

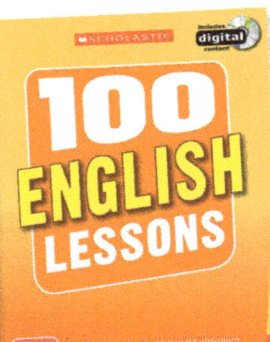

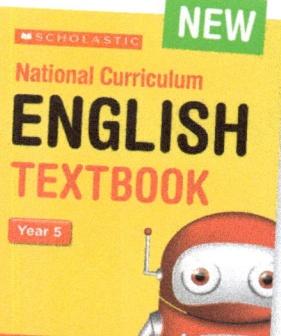

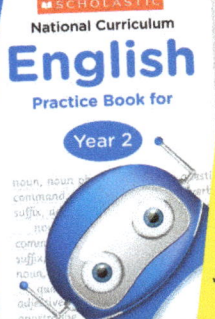

Planning | Lessons | Textbooks | Practice | Assessment

scholastic.co.uk/textbooks